Unforgettable Kalimpong

Monila De

notionpress.com

INDIA · SINGAPORE · MALAYSIA

Notion Press

Old No. 38, New No. 6
McNichols Road, Chetpet
Chennai - 600 031

First Published by Notion Press 2018

ISBN 978-1-64324-662-8

To

Baruna for encouraging me and Elizabeth for burning the midnight oil, in deciphering my illegible hand writing and typing it out.

"A happy childhood can't be cured. Mine will hang around my neck like a rainbow, that's all, instead of a noose."

– Hortens Calisher

Contents

Foreword

Why Kalimpong?

There were two main reasons why we came to live in Kalimpong. One was the Second World War and the second, the death of my elder sister, Monjula.

We lived through most of the war in Calcutta as my fifteen year old sister was bedridden with tuberculosis and couldn't be moved. All those who could have gone had already left.

Two events took place almost simultaneously. My sister, Monjula, died and the Japanese army managed to drop a bomb in *Hatibagan,* close to our house in Calcutta. It was too close for comfort, but baba refused to move out of Calcutta. He was not going to leave his hearth and home and flee.

He was counting on Subash Chandra Bose who had joined hands with the Japanese to come and deliver us from British bondage. The other families did not have such faith in Subash Bose. They panicked and there was a mass exodus to nearby places Giridhi, Hazaribag, etc.

Calcutta became a ghost city. Curfews, sirens wailing day and night. Glass paned windows criss-crossed with paper strips, to keep them from shattering in a blast. Blackouts were the worst. Every time the sirens wailed after dark, all lights had to be switched off and everyone made a mad rush to the bomb shelter on the ground floor.

A small, dark, windowless room, damp and airless. A room with reinforced walls to offer protection against falling

Japanese bombs. We huddled here in agonizing silence till the all clear was sounded and everyone bounded back to life again.

I was not afraid at all. It was a huge game for me. I was only three years old, the danger and gravity of the situation was far beyond my understanding.

Ma had already given baba an ultimatum that she was not going to live in Calcutta anymore, after my sister's death. She had lost a beautiful, talented daughter in the prime of her life and she was going to lose me in the same way, if we lived here any longer. She was not going to bring me up in the pollution-ridden city of Calcutta at any cost. She insisted that baba should find a hill station in the nearby Himalayas with clear, cool air where I could be brought up without any chance of catching the dreaded, incurable disease, T.B.

Baba still under shock, of losing his beloved daughter, gave in to ma's ultimatum and went to look for such a place in the Himalayas. Darjeeling he found too cold and wet. Kurseong, Mungpo, Takda, Pedong were not at all suitable. He then landed in Kalimpong and fell in love with it. It was the ideal place for us he decided.

The danger that a skirmish with the Japanese force posed was upper most in everyone's mind but what hastened baba's decision to move us out of Calcutta was machine gun patter, one Sunday afternoon.

Guests and our whole family were relaxing in our large drawing room after lunch, chewing *paan* contentedly after a belly full of sumptuous lunch, a rare treat at a time of shortage and rationing. When the sirens blared no one made a move to rush down to the bomb shelter. The siren was crying wolf far too often. Nobody was in a rush to sit in the dungeon like bomb shelter in deadly silence.

Among the guests was a close family friend, a Major in the British army, on a short home leave. In the distance we heard the muffled boom of cannon fire. The crows sent up a cacophony in fright followed by an eerie calm. The Major rushed to the verandah, we followed with bated breath. The sun shone brightly in the clear blue sky; there was no sign of Japanese bombers but high up hung three round puffs of white smoke.

The soldier now had a chance to display his knowledge of war fare. "No, we cannot delay any longer. We must take shelter underground," he declared in panic. He grabbed me in his arms and rushed down to the bomb shelter. The others followed suit. The minute we reached the shelter the siren wailed, all clear. All eyes alighted on the red faced experienced soldier.

This is all I remember about what was taking place in Calcutta. The young Major, after the cannon fire fiasco, felt it was imperative to boost his flagging ego by divulging inside secrets about the war to baba in a loud whisper. "The Japanese have already captured Singapore and Burma. They are stationed in the Andaman Islands and will be here soon. Calcutta is their main target. They will raise it to the ground. Get out before it is too late," he warned.

Baba was a practical man, he was unfazed by rumors, cannon shots or even the bombs but he felt uncomfortable about the inside knowledge the Major claimed to have. He had just lost a grown up daughter and now he did not want to jeopardize me and my mother's life. He decided to move us to Kalimpong at once.

Introduction

In the year 1941, a little girl left her home in war time Calcutta, not only to escape the blackouts, sirens, the sandbags and the trenches, but also to soothe a personal grief.

She came with her mother to the small, secure, serene Himalayan town of Kalimpong and here she has stayed.

Kalimpong whose name in the local Lepcha language means "Ridges where we play," was indeed at the time a meeting point if not a playground for many people from the world over. It was an entre-port for Indo-Tibetan trade, a sanctuary for exiled royalty, a canvas for aspiring artists, a starting point for Himalayan expeditions and pied a Terre firma for naturalists who travelled far to discover the wealth of flora and fauna of the region.

Young Monila's gregarious nature and inborn curiosity helped her to be acquainted with a wonderful mixture of people and places in her new home, see them in a kaleidoscope of shapes and colours and a concert of sounds which delighted her and stayed impressed in her memory to be later transformed into charming word pictures.

And the result is this very readable collection of stories – funny, sad, romantic and even bizarre, keeping always in tune with the spirit of Kalimpong.

– Bunny Gupta

Ma and me in the train toilet

Kalimpong 1941

After much packing, loaded with luggage, ma and I were off to Kalimpong at last. We boarded the Darjeeling Mail at Sealdah Station. Baba came to see us off. Moina, my ayah and Suren the cook were to travel in the attendant's compartment right next to our first class one.

This was not my first train journey but this is the one I remember very clearly although I was only three years old. The compartment was like a well-furnished room with five wide berths in green leather upholstery. The polished wood work shone in the dim light. The cemented green floor matched the green upholstery. It was quite grand.

Now that we were well settled in the compartment, baba was giving ma last minute instructions. I grew restless and decided to use the toilet. Ma showed me the narrow door but didn't accompany me. I inspected the tiny toilet leisurely. It was spotlessly clean. The brass tap shone atop a small basin with a mirror above it. The English commode with a polished wooden seat was too high for me. I looked in and was shocked to find a gaping hole. I would never be found if I fell into it! The safest option was to relieve myself near the opening in the floor.

Ma came in to pull the flush. She saw the little puddle on the polished green floor. "What have you done?" she shrieked in horror. "You are supposed to sit on the potty, not on the floor, you stupid girl. What will the English ladies think of you? They will think you are a little *Junglee native.*" With that she rushed out to find paper to dry the floor. I was mortified and learned very early in life, to do as the British do, so as not to be branded as an ignorant native!

Ma and I occupied the middle berth while the two on either side next to the windows were occupied by two very old, fat English ladies, clad in white night gowns and bonnets. Only their colourless blubbery faces were visible, cheeks jiggling as the train picked up speed. They looked exactly alike. I kept turning my head from one to the other to find if there was an iota of dissimilarity between them until, ma glared at me to stop me from staring at them.

These two lay prostrate all through the journey attended by a smart young nurse, in a starched white uniform with matching cap, stockings and rubber soled shoes. She was busy doling out pills and potions to them. Tucking them in and making them as comfortable as possible.

A smartly dressed bearer arrived wearing a green turban with a matching broad belt. A huge, highly polished monogrammed brass clasp shone in the middle of his belly. His white long coat and pant were spotless. I was much impressed by his get up, compared to our *dhuti,* clad servants, he was a knight in shining armour.

To ma all food cooked outside her home reeked with T.B. Germs. She was obsessed with them because her beloved daughter had died of that dreaded incurable disease. She had therefore carried a tiffin carrier full of food, enough for two days.

The bearer had to be satisfied with just one order of dinner from the young nurse. Soon a tray laden with a sumptuous meal arrived for her. I couldn't take my eyes off the tray with shining cutlery, starched white napkin and mouth watering food. Again ma's eyes round and disapproving sent a clear message, "Don't stare." The nurse ate hungrily while I picked disgustedly at an egg sandwich.

The morning brought the wonders of a train journey. The shutters had been up all night to stop all, real or imaginary, drafts that would have troubled the old ladies. Now, I could see the country side through the clear glass panes. Trees rushed passed in a terrific hurry. The telephone lines with rows of little birds dipped and then suddenly rose up to meet the next pole.

The rhythmic clickity-clack of the wheels rose to a crescendo as the train thundered on. The sharp bursts of whistle from the monstrous engine added to the music, in its urgency to reach its destination in record time.

The carriage heaved and rocked threatening to bounce off the two old ladies from their bunks. Their medicine bottles, flasks swayed and clinked ready to fly off their perches any minute. Oh, it was such fun to be transported at such speed with the train's very special brand of rocketing rock music. So much noise inside while silent pictures of the countryside were momentarily framed in the window.

At last we arrived at Siliguri station. The morning sun beat down on a dusty strip of platform with an awning. Turbaned *coolies* in red shirts and *dhutis,* clamoured to carry our luggage to the taxi.

I was bundled into a huge taxi of American make with thick well padded seats, excellent for bouncing on. The air inside was stifling. It was a powerful mixture of stale sweat, petrol fumes and vomit which impregnated the upholstery and had tenaciously clung to it for years. The windows were too small to let in much air to dispel this nauseating smell.

As we reached the mountains, we drove through a dark tunnel of trees. Sunlight couldn't penetrate this dark green canopy to reach the bumpy, unmetalled dark, damp road with sharp twists and turns. The damp forest produced a very pecial smell of its own, of rotting vegetation. It was the most overpowering, stomach churning, vilest smell I had ever inhaled. It enveloped my whole mind and body. I could stand it no longer; out spewed my breakfast in a rush all over the faded seats like many before me.

These horrifying smells remained with me all through my childhood.

The very thought of making this journey but twice a year, made me a nervous wreck every time the date of travel drew near.

Mercifully the rocking of the well sprung car lulled me to sleep. Ma woke me up as we neared our destination, Kanchanjungha *Kothi* high up in the hill of West Rickshaw Road, where baba had rented a small flat for us to stay. My sleep laden eyes caught a fleeting glimpse of a gurgling *'jhora'* as we sped over a bridge with solid iron railings. I learnt later, that this bridge was called *Bansuri Pool* because the *jhora,* flowing under it sounded like music coming from a flute. On both banks of the *jhora,* rows of long, white, bell like flowers *dhatura* or the devil's trumpet danced in the breeze under a clear blue sky and bright sun. This was my first glimpse of Kalimpong.

Kanchanjungha Kothi

Kanchanjungha *Kothi,* what an apt name for a house, as it faced the magnificent Kanchanjungha. It was a conglomeration of bungalows and servant's quarters owned by Mrs. David Mohan, universally known as *Phupu.*

Numerous people lived here of various shapes, sizes, ages, castes and creeds. I was now the youngest member of this township, therefore, made much of and spoilt by everybody.

Phupu, was the first person in Kalimpong to let out portions of her large bungalow and out houses as flats. This she did out of necessity, being widowed at the age of twenty six. Not that she was poor by any means, she owned plenty of land and property but letting out portions of her house meant ready cash. This she required for her charity work and lavish entertaining. Our two bed roomed flat with dining cum sitting room cost Rs. 20/- per month and ours was the largest flat.

Phupu, was a lady of enormous proportions, the largest human being that I had ever seen! Her moon like face was always wreathed in smiles, her lap more comfortable and cozier than any Dunlop pillow on which I was hoisted very often.

The all enveloping *saree* which so conveniently and generously conceals all imperfections in a woman's body, did not hide her girth. Simply because *Phupu,* did not wear it in its conventional form but wrapped it around her waist, pleated in front like a voluminous skirt, held by a cummerbund. Her silk, long sleeved blouse tucked into it. Her thinning hair was mostly covered by a huge, white, triangular scarf. This was the Nepali dress.

What fascinated me most was her jewellery that she donned for formal occasions. The enormous gold discs for earrings which threatened to tear off her earlobes, a matching but much larger gold breast plate of a locket which sat in the middle of her bosom.

Phupu's voice was amazingly thin, soft and soothing emanating from such a corpulent body. She only spoke Nepali, Lepcha and Hindi. She could understand both Bengali and English. She conversed with the British in Hindi whether they understood her or not. She was the undisputed queen of Kalimpong and the matriarch of her private domain, Kanchanjunga *Kothi.*

Her constant companion was *'Sanu,' Phupu,* literally a small *Phupu,* was diametrically opposite to *Phupu,* not only in size but temperamentally as well. She was always neatly garbed in white, with only, her equally white face visible. Her eyes were mere slits and it was very difficult to decipher whether they were open or shut. They were actually forever open and through these slits, she noted everything and everyone, especially all their misdeeds and lapses. None could avoid her keen eyes or her razor sharp tongue. Everyone gave her a wide berth, so did I.

Apart from *Sanu Phupu, Phupu's* family consisted of her nephew Khaisa and niece Sunkumari. Khaisa was a dark, slim, shy young man with a mass of black woolly hair. Sunkumari was a restless teenager with a disposition as bright as the sun, she was named after. A tomboy who preferred to run wild rather than concentrate on her studies.

There was no one of her age group to play with so I became her living doll. She ran up hill and down bouncing me on her back. I loved these excursions. She was a fun person to be with, play with. She became my firm friend and companion in spite of our age difference.

Haldar was *Phupu*'s head cook and adopted son. Apart from his cooking chores he always accompanied *Phupu,* helping her in and out of the only taxi which sank every time she boarded it! He was married to a young Lepcha woman but they were issueless, I turned out to be a good substitute.

Haldar was a man of short stature. What added to his height and distinguished him from all others was his embossed, black Nepali hat with a small pom-pom on top. It sat like a four pound cake on his head. He wore these hats all through his life and was even buried in one. He was the lord and master of the servant's domain.

An elderly man with a shining bald pate took his morning constitutional in the back yard, wrapped in a maroon, shiny silk dressing gown, spangled with a maze of bright yellow tendrils and flowers. The silent old man kept to himself. His stock question, whenever he saw me watching him curiously, was "Khuku how are you?" he did not expect a reply as he walked on briskly without stopping and none was forth coming from me.

The Anglo-Indian family who lived above his flat was strange. They strictly kept to themselves; we were natives after all and beneath their dignity to hob-nob with. Their two little boys of five and six were not allowed to speak to anybody and they shunned all my advances to play with them. They scampered off as soon as they saw me. So my only companion was Sunkumari *didi* whom I adored.

The father of the two boys was a bullet headed young man with sandy crew cut hair. His faded blue eyes, colourless thin face was expressionless. He always wore short sleeved shirts and baggy half pants. Early every morning, he set off purposefully with his net down to the Teesta River to catch butterflies. As for his wife, I would catch a glimpse of her puffy, white, sad face at their window sometimes.

The small flat next to ours was occupied by a slim Swedish lady with white hair. Miss Onsul was far from old but anybody with white hair, to me, was ancient. She was from Sweden and lived in Kalimpong to avoid the heat of the plains. She became quite friendly with ma. After Independence when Pandit Nehru became the first prime minister of India and lived in Teen Murti, Miss Onsul was appointed by him as his house keeper. In later years, whenever we visited New Delhi, she invited us to Teen Murti for tea.

The rectangular back yard, hemmed in by buildings was an ideal play field for all and sundry. Its constant use never allowed any grass to grow on it. A sandy patch with sharp stones on which I regularly grazed my knees and hands. The greatest fun enjoyed by Khaisa *daju*, servants and visiting children including me, was a game of football on it. In the absence of a real football, the *pumelos*, as big as a regular football, from the tall *pumelo* tree, near the drive, was an excellent substitute. The *pumelos* were too acidic for consumption, only fit for playing football.

Kanchanjunga *Kothi* was a beehive of activity with scores of people coming to visit *Phupu*, every day. Peoples visit to Kalimpong would be incomplete without meeting the queen of Kalimpong. Friends, relatives and all VIP's were regularly invited for sumptuous meals at *Phupu's* who was a charming, gracious, extremely hospitable hostess and made everybody feel at home.

Kanchanjunga *Kothi* was a wonderful place where everybody lived happily absolutely untouched by the Second World War raging all around the world. It was *Phupu's,* exclusive and private domain, a melting pot of cultures, religion and race. All those who visited Kalimpong and met *Phupu,* never forgot her.

Queen of Hearts

From my three years old height and eyes, *Phupu* looked enormous, and so she was. Always neatly dressed in traditional Nepali clothes and a solid gold necklace that sat on her bosom, she looked imposing and grand.

Often she would sit me on her spacious lap. I would get lost in the pleats of her *guneu.*

Ma was inconsolable at the loss of her elder daughter Monjula. *Phupu,* turned out to be just the right person to lift ma out of her depression and sorrow by her compassion, sympathy and kindness.

Large hearted and generous to a fault, her mission in life seemed to be, to help the distressed. When her brother and his wife died leaving five orphaned children, she adopted them immediately and brought them up as her own.

They called her *Phupu,* so everybody took to calling her *Phupu,* including her tenant farmers, only recently I got to know her real name, Azem Rebecca Mohan. Others called her David *Babuni.* Mr. David Mohan from the plains was a *Babu* in a tea garden in Darjeeling; so naturally, being his wife she was called a *Babuni.*

Sunkumari didi found me feeding the young kid *Phupu* had given me, with toast and jam, she thought it was hilarious. Kids ate grass not bread and jam! In later years when she had children of her own this became their oft repeated bed time story. The children referred to me as the aunt who fed the goat with toast and jam.

Sunkumari *didi*, was my sole companion whom I loved dearly. Out of the blue arrived, a smug little Anglo-Nepalese boy called Mulukchand. Soon Sunkumari *didi*, was completely engrossed with him and paid scant attention to me. I was hurt and upset. Just to spite the pretentious young brat, I named my kid Mulukchand!

Her eldest brother John was in the army. He arrived home on leave. Handsome, smartly dressed in his army uniform, he took my breath away. I fell in love with him instantly and declared to all and sundry that I was going to marry him when I grew up, to everyone's amusement.

Phupu's doors were open to all nationalities, from all walks of life. She could only speak Nepali, Lepcha and broken Hindi. Once *Phupu* met people, language became secondary. Her warmth and charm sliced through all barriers and won their hearts forever.

The snobbish British gentry visited her regularly. The young ladies came to have their palms read. Dr. Graham visited her often on horseback all the way from the Homes. She was not only invited to the British homes but no important parties for governors or other VIPs would be complete without her.

She in turn threw the most lavish tea, lunch and dinner parties, almost one every week, not only for permanent residents but everyone who stepped into Kalimpong for a short visit.

Since there was no restriction about children attending these parties, I always accompanied ma. I was a fussy and poor eater but I would starve myself all day to do justice to her delicious fare.

The tables would be laden with western, Chinese, Nepali and Indian dishes. Each item cooked to perfection by Haldar, her super cook. He had been adopted by *Phupu,* at the age of nine. Being a smart young lad, he picked up his cooking skills from the expert *Baburchis* who came from the British houses to cook for *Phupu's* big parties. He turned out to be a marvellous cook. Quite famous in Kalimpong. His soufflés were just out of this world.

Not endowed with a sweet tooth, I would shun all puddings but his soufflés I couldn't resist! *Phupu,* aware of my weakness, would hand me the soufflé bowl after the guests had their fill, to lick it clean.

She loved to cook. She would sit in front of the charcoal *chula,* on a wide, sturdy stool and enjoy cooking for hours. She modified or created new dishes taking her guests on a delightful, scintillating, gastronomic journey, titillating their taste buds to heights of ecstasy.

Her parties were not only a gourmand's delight but a most enjoyable social event. Her face beaming with good humour, eyes twinkling with merriment, she would regale her guests with stories about herself that kept them in splits of laughter.

She had a rare sense of humour. Baba always kidded her about her unusual size. He advised her to eat less. Fed up by his friendly jibes, she said, "Mitra Sahib even just drinking water makes one fat!" This remark amused baba so much that he never badgered her again.

One naive lady from Calcutta asked her why the people of the hills had rather flat rounded features. "You see, we live high up in the mountains, closer to the sun which melts down the sharp features," she answered.

She would relate her life story which started with her being married at the age of 14 to Mr. David Mohon, a man of 60, old enough to be her grandfather. After her wedding she came to her husband's house in a *doli* along with her favourite dolls.

Hers was an arranged marriage. Mr. Mohon was married to her aunt. When she died, he expressed a desire to marry again. The family intended to keep this old man and his wealth in their clutches so hurriedly decided to give him *Phupu,* being the only scapegoat available.

She had not received any formal education, so her grandfather of a spouse set about educating her. A cranky old man he had no patience with his child bride. Tired of his constant bickering, one day, in a fit of rage, she tore up all her books, put the pencils, rubbers etc, tied them in a bundle and flung it out of the window. To evade her husband's wrath she nimbly climbed up the tallest tree, sat on the highest branch until her husband beseeched her to come down on condition not to teach her any more. Thus ended her education.

It was a mystery to me how a lady of her proportions ever climbed a tree, leave alone reaching the highest branch. It occurred to me much later that she must have been slight and lissome at 14.

After 15 years of issueless married life Mr. Mohon died leaving her a huge fortune. The rich young widow owned all the land from below Morgan house down to the two houses Nilachal and Suktara. She sold these two houses. The kindly missionaries to lighten her burden sold all the land above Kanchanjunga Kothi at Rs. 20/- per decimal... (roughly 450 sq ft). She also owned great tracts of paddy land and orange orchards in the villages.

A cunning and ambitions fortune hunter lured by her riches arrived to woo her. She entertained him with proper decorum and courtesy, not suspecting his devious intentions but the minute he proposed to her, she flew into a fearful rage, picked up the nearest walking stick and thrashed him until he fled stumbling down the stairs in a mighty hurry never to return!

The missionaries alarmed by the possibility of more fortune hunters coming to woo the young widow whisked her off to *Lal Kothi.* Now Girls High School.

She might have stayed under their care permanently but for one fatal mistake they made. They tried to educate her. Very soon she was back in Kanchanjunga *Kothi* where she lived and died.

It was highly improper and dangerous the missionaries thought for a young widow to live alone so they promptly sent a companion for her. Miss Youngzen, a young Lepcha school teacher. She turned out to be the absolute antithesis of *Phupu.* A slim, slight petit lady always dressed in white with a disposition far from genial. She became *Sanu Phupu,* to all. Unsmiling and strict she could peer at us through mere slits for eyes, spotting every mischief we were up to.

Sanu Phupu, set about teaching *Phupu,* all the intricacies of socializing and entertaining in proper British style which she had picked up from them. *Phupu,* didn't need much training in either department. A born hostess, with no airs and graces, she put people at ease immediately. She loved people, her simplicity and sincerity won them over.

Whenever Rabindra Nath Tagore visited Gouripur house, she would go to meet and invite him for a meal. Being of poor health he always declined but asked her to invite his secretary instead.

Her ordinary parties were lavish but Christmas parties were spectacular. The festivities lasted for a week. The whole house was decorated with streamers, balloons and bunches of blood-red poinsettias. On Christmas eve close friends and VIPs were invited then everyone in turn. The tables groaned with delectable delicacies.

On Christmas day after attending church she would treat the villagers to a sumptuous meal. After the meal she would give little presents to the children and send food for the ones who were incapable of attending the party due to old age or ill health.

She kept a food stall at the *mela* ground, for the yearly *mela*. The British flocked to her stall for the delicious Indian food and soon everything was sold out. The money collected at the *mela*, went to the British soldiers.

There were other attractions at the *mela*, too. One sports day *Phupu*, was game enough to run a three-legged race with Raja Dorji as her partner. She half carried the slim Raja most of the way to the amusement of the crowd.

Phupu was uneducated but very intelligent; she could barely sign her name in English. She was simple but far from a simpleton. She ran her estate very efficiently. She was the first person in Kalimpong to start the flat system. She would discuss legal matters with Madan Babu cleverly. She even started a soap factory and sold milk, not so much to make money but to give jobs to poor people.

Generous to a fault, she would never turn anyone away who came to her for help. She would distribute rice to the poor and needy. People came to her not only for help but advice as well; including government officials. She became the undisputed "First lady" of Kalimpong.

She was nominated to be the municipality commissioner, later on when elections started for the post, she won hands down.

She was the champion of the Lepcha cause. She became the first President of the Lepcha association in 1947. She took a Lepcha delegation to New Delhi to meet Pandit Nehru. He was charmed by her. She also took Lepcha groups to Calcutta for cultural shows. She helped in making the first documentary film on Lepchas. Unfortunately it cannot be traced now. She encouraged people to write books in the Lepcha language. She was the one to demand and got tribal status for the Lepchas.

To her dismay she found Lepchas selling off their ancestral land to non-Lepchas. They would lose their identity along with their land she thought. To stop this practice she managed to get the authorities to pass a law by which Lepchas could only sell their land to other Lepchas.

Her heart went out to those poor deprived Lepcha families so she would give them a treat often. She would take them to the Novelty Cinema Hall to watch Bioscope, take them to Siliguri or Darjeeling for a day's picnic. All her acts of kindness endeared her to the rich, powerful and the lowly.

Although we had built and shifted to our house, Monjula, ma visited her very often. She encouraged ma in her social work. I couldn't accompany her as I was attending school but invitations to *Phupu's* parties I wouldn't miss for the world.

The gentle lady's temper was well known, once she had slapped the local Sub Divisional British Officer and got away with it, fortunately *Phupu's* temper surfaced rarely. It surfaced once again for the last time.

Her favorite niece Sunkumari, the tomboy, had blossomed into a vivacious charming young lady. Her greatest crime was falling in love with the most eligible bachelor in town. Well educated, young and very handsome, a Christian to boot but not a Lepcha. Mr. P.R. Pradhan presented himself in front of *Phupu,* to ask for her niece's hand in marriage. She flew into a royal rage and ordered him out, he was lucky not to have met the same fate as *Phupu's* suitor, years ago!

With no other option the young couple eloped. *Phupu* hurt and angry refused to see them ever again.

Suffering from prolonged illness she passed away in 1965. She is remembered with affection and her memories remain evergreen in the hearts of all those who were privileged to have known her. She was the undisputed Queen of Hearts.

Superman Bahadur

Bahadur entered my life and changed it completely. Sunkumari *didi* was my only friend and companion till Bahadur came along. A short sturdy lad of sixteen with black wavy hair, a wide nose atop his flat round face, twinkling mischievous eyes, dressed in khaki shorts and white shirt stood at our door one morning. He had been sent by *Phupu*, to ma for employment.

Ma was quite content with Suren the cook and Moina the ayah, she didn't need an extra pair of hands. She was about to tell him just that when his bright eager face made her change her mind and she appointed him for a monthly salary of Rupees 5/-. His only job would be to keep me company. Ma found his name Ratna Bahadur Mukhia, a mouthful so she called him by his middle name Bahadur.

Bahadur spoke no Bengali and I no Nepali but very soon I picked it up from him perfectly, including the choicest swear words. He opened up a whole new world for me, the world of nature. Every morning he would take me for long rambles. He would run nimbly, surefooted as a mountain goat with me bouncing on his back, down the steep *chor batos* even though there were no *chors,* in Kalimpong then.

Pristine Kalimpong with thick forests, gurgling *jhoras* bouncing down the hillside under lush green foliage of white trumpet flowers, smooth green hill side, tall thick bamboo groves, orange orchards and a few thatched huts down in the valley. During the monsoons the rice fields full of water in the valley mirrored the sky and then turned bright green. The distant, ageless, indigo mountain ranges stood still. Their crowning glory, Kanchanjungha. It was paradise.

In spring, the hill sides were full of ripe, sweet raspberries. We would gorge on these, then slake our thirst by drinking sparkling water from cool mountain springs. We hardly used the smooth black metalled roads that circled Kalimpong but sometimes used the roadside stone benches to rest.

A long row of benches in a lonely spot, around a wide bend in the road, was where the beautiful churels, gathered every night to lure unsuspecting young men. "What if a *churel,* catches you?" I asked Bahadur, alarmed at the prospect of losing him to a *churel.* "Don't worry Khuku, I will never be caught by a *churel,* I am too smart for them. First I will feel her back which is hollow, just a skeleton and then look at her feet which are always turned backwards." I would heave a sigh of relief.

Bahadur had a very fertile imagination. Totally unlettered, he would find an explanation for everything he saw and heard and I became his sounding board. "Khuku, you see that pebble there, well, it will grow and grow into one of those mountains one day," for many years I believed that stones grew like all living things.

"When a banana plant is cut in half, water drips from it. The people in the desert have no water so they use it for drinking." He had found a use for the water in banana plant without realizing that they don't grow in deserts. "Since they have no water there they use sand to clean their utensils." This was perhaps true. "Khuku, the muscular man who passed us is the strongest man in Kalimpong. He can lift a cow. He started by lifting a calf every day. He got so used to it that he can now lift it even though it is a full grown cow! Just see what practice does."

Bahadur was anti-management; he admired the cooks, bearers and ayahs who had got the better of their mistresses. He would tell me numerous such stories. An old English spinster, suspected her cook of pilfering bread so she walked into the kitchen when he was slicing a loaf, on a board, in front of an open window. The wily cook kept on slicing deftly, flicking alternate slices with the tip of his knife out of the window. The memsahib, with poor eye sight, was unable to spot the slices flying out of the window. She was well satisfied and felt guilty for doubting the cook for stealing.

Bahadur was always kind and gentle with me, a happy young lad with an appalling temper. During these temper tantrums; he was capable of smashing and destroying anything at hand. The following escapade of a young bearer in a British household, gave him enormous pleasure and he repeated it often.

The memsahib had used her priceless old crockery at a special party. She asked her bearer to store it all carefully in the glass display cabinet. In spite of extreme care and caution, the bearer managed to crack a serving dish. It was only a hairline crack and he hoped his mistress wouldn't detect it. She did and flew into a right royal rage. The poor bearer tried to reason with her. "It is only a slight crack memsahib; it is whole and not broken in two. It can be used again." it was beyond him to fathom that a crack was as good as being broken and the set had lost its value.

The memsahib refused to accept any apology or explanation. She gave him the sack. The bearer had enough of her raving and ranting over a silly China dish. He packed up his bags and just before he left, he walked into the dining room quietly and gave the glass display cabinet a hefty push. "Serves her right Khuku, isn't it?" Bahadur would laugh, gloating and admiring the audacity of sacked bearer.

Bahadur disliked the *baidars,* and *defadors* of the *coolies.* "They are all slave drivers, you know Khuku, they are harsh and mean to the *coolies.*" he would utter in disgust. He even encouraged them to rebel against their tormentors. His theory was, no matter the short comings of the employees which included lying, stealing, damaging property, disobedience and indiscipline, they should never be chastised or punished, or the consequences could be disastrous. Bahadur would have made an excellent labour Union leader.

Bahadur was a great entertainer and all his stories were action packed specially the ghost stories that he made up. The other stories were hearsays like these. Kaila Kami had stolen his neighbour's prized cock. The neighbour complained to the village elders. They ordered Kaila to return the cock or compensate him. The irate neighbour wanted neither. All he wanted was a fit punishment for the *chor.* He spelt out the punishment he thought fit. All he wanted was to defect on the *chor's* face in public.

The elders suggested several punishments far worse than that but the man was adamant. Exasperated the elders declared, "Yes old man, you can defect on his face." The old man was delighted until he heard the rest of the sentence. "Of course, you can defect on his face if you choose but during the process, not a single drop of urine must fall on him." The old man flabbergasted at this judgment went home grumbling at the impossibility of this task. Much later I realized that the story was the simplified village version of Merchant of Venice.

"You know Khuku, pickpockets learn their trade at a special school. This is how they are taught by their teacher. He takes a small tin can, puts a purse in it and wraps a wad of acid soaked rag around the rim of the can. Then asks his pupils to pick out the purse without touching the rag which will burn their fingers. Once they have mastered the art of picking pockets deftly, they are sent out by him to earn a living. This must be another watered down version of Charles Dickens's artful Dodger."

As I grew older, ghost stories replaced these stories. His fertile imagination could conjure up the most terrifying ghosts who would send shivers up my spine but thrilled me no end. I was not afraid of them either because he had given me a charmed pen knife which would protect me from all evil spirits.

one evening some of ma's friends had come visiting with her children. Bahadur delighted to have an audience gave his best action packed performance, of his choicest ghost stories to entertain them. The children listened wide eyed and spell bound, asking for more. The next day the mothers of these children arrived to complain to ma, "That Bahadur should never be allowed to tell ghost stories to the children they had nightmares all night long."

Hardly any toys were available in Kalimpong. Those that were didn't interest me specifically, the Bakelite dolls I received as presents. They were the exact replicas of the British *babas*. Bahadur, to keep me occupied, fashioned toys out of wood, bamboos, rubber, branches from trees. Useful toys that worked were pea shooters, catapults, kites, flutes etc. A *khukuri* and a penknife were his only tools. I soon learnt to make them too, honing my motor skills in the process.

I would cut myself often but running to ma bleeding, crying for medication and sympathy, was out of the question. She would immediately put an end to all such activities. Bhahadur would stop the bleeding miraculously by applying a crushed weed that grew in the garden. Soon I was using the *khukuri,* with expertise and carried a small one of my own to every adult's anxiety.

Bahadur disliked the *gora* soldiers for making passes at the *kanchis* but he admired their uniforms and their highly polished hob nailed boots. He considered these the ultimate in men's attire and longed to own them. I, on the other hand longed to wear shorts and shirts like him. When I asked ma for such a set, she was horrified. "Little girls don't wear shorts and shirt; you have such pretty frocks." But I was adamant and soon a set arrived from the tailor.

I loved the comfort and freedom of these clothes. They were much easier for climbing trees and running around rather than those silly fancy frocks. The next thing I discarded were my fancy shoes. it was far easier to go barefoot. now I was miniature Bahadur except for my shoulder length hair. The hajam, used to come to Kanchanjungha Kothi once a month to cut the men's hair and shave them. I wanted him to cut my hair as short as Bahadur's but ma put her foot down.

The *rotiwala* with his tin trunk stuck on top of his to head, an extension of his body, came every day with his goodies. Everybody crowded around to buy mouth-watering freshly baked items but I was forbidden to eat any of it. If anybody offered me a morsel, Bahadur would whisper, "Don't take it, it is *jutho.*" He did not allow me to eat anything in front of other children either. "They will put *chokhay* on your food." This meant that if somebody desired my food and didn't get it, I was sure to get severe gripes he said. He was always so protective of me.

Bahadur couldn't read or write but he had picked up the English alphabet and numbers which he taught me. This came in handy when I joined school; I was the only child who knew them. He taught himself to read Bengali and English. There were many teething problems in our new house once we moved in. He learnt to fix leaking taps to more complicated repairs. He even learnt to fix machinery. To me he was Superman. He could do anything except fly.

Eventually he graduated to cooking. He had picked up several recipies from Haldar at Kanchanjunga Kothi. Ma taught him the rest. He turned our excellent dishes, that is, if he followed a recipe meticulously but most often, his imagination ran wild and he would experiment with bizarre combinations which hit the jackpot sometime and inedible at others.

Ma was always on tenter hooks when she invited people, not knowing what new dish he would produce. Fish with apple stuffing, pineapple fish curry, chocolate in meat curry, roast chicken with bananas and corn stuffing, leg of mutton with *dal* sauce. He would be hailed as a super chef today for his innovative fusion dishes. I also learnt basic cooking skills from him but I never have the guts or imagination to experiment with mixing and matching as boldly as he did.

Now that cooking was taking up all his time, he had no time to entertain me. I was lonely in the evenings, after I returned from school, that is when the football fellows came to my rescue. I would play football and then sit on the kitchen stool and watch him cooking dinner and telling him about my day. He was the only one I enjoyed talking to. In front of others I was shy and tongue tied. I only liked his company and none other.

Bahadur married our maid *Kanchi*, an ugly woman, much older than him with a son in tow. Soon they produced a son whom I loved dearly. He was my living doll. He was a lovely little fellow. I carried him around on my back as his father used to carry me, repeat all the stories Bahadur used to tell me and taught him all the skills I had learnt from him, so the circle was now complete.

Moina

Ma had brought Moina, my ayah, from Calcutta. She was originally from Krishnagar where all ayahs came from. A dark, serene, young women with the sculptured, ebony face of a Madonna with the temper of a tigress. Her head of black hair covered by the long *anchal,* of a blue bordered, white *saree,* with only her face visible, was a picture of tranquility and innocence. All those who visited our house specially, the men, were struck by her beauty and grace of her lissome body.

All these qualities of hers were lost on me. Behind ma's back, she was nasty, mean and rude to me. I was too young to fight back or complain to ma. Disobedience of not complying with her strict routine of bathing, dressing, eating and afternoon sleep was quickly quelled by threats of the *jujuburis* and *pethnis,* who relished devouring little girls like me.

Her main aim was to put me to sleep, each afternoon, as soon as possible, so that she could retire to the kitchen for her lunch and gossip session. Any delay by me, would drive her into a frenzy and threats of *bhooths, pethnis* and *jujuburis,* with enormous humps, would descend on me fast and furious.

Waking up from my afternoon sleep, I was hurriedly dressed and made to gulp down a silver glass full of milk which I detested and resisted. This was met with a vigorous shaking, curdling the milk in my stomach. Moina's aim now, was not only to take me for my evening walk but to join the ayahs with their wards for another gossip session.

The meeting place of the ayahs of the locality was at the bifurcation of West Rickshaw Road and Upper Cart Road. This provided a large play field for their wards with a long stone bench which was an ideal perch for them. at the end of the bench stood a red, cast iron letter box, bearing the imperial crown. The bench still stands but the heavy iron letter box, the last relic of the British era, has fallen prey to greedy *bikriwalas.*

This wide road was perfectly safe as no cars ever drove through since, there were hardly any cars in Kalimpong. An occasionally army jeep or trucks full of tomato faced British soldiers drove past and the ayahs would spring up to gather their *babas,* from imminent disaster. Sometimes Sahibs and Memsahibs would canter pass on their horses to visit friends.

Most interesting of all were the huge rickshaws. A regular horse drawn carriage without the horses. They were drawn by four strong Tibetan young men, dressed in *bokhus* and knee high colourful Tibetan boots. Their hair hung down in long plaits. These rickshaws were used by elderly passengers, dressed in their finery to go visiting.

I disliked these daily excursions but Moina loved them, in spite of the British appointed ayahs looking down on her and often making fun of her. They considered themselves a cut above her, being better paid and proud of serving their white memsahibs. She was on the last rung of the pecking order.

Moina was a woman of few words and was no match for them. Yet she longed for their company. I suppose it gave her a sense of belonging amongst her own kind. Of course what she enjoyed most was the gossip. These ayahs sat cross legged on the bench, like bloated frogs with wide open, *pan,* stained, red lips, displaying corroded black teeth, blaring out outrageous tales about their British masters and mistresses.

I hated the colourless *babas* of all shapes and sizes with hair of all colours ranging from white to flaming orange. Their pale eyes too, looked like marbles of many hues. They ganged up against me since I was the odd one out. The spoilt monsters struck out their tongues, pulled my hair, made horrible faces and resorted to several devices to tease and torture me. Moina, too engrossed, in juicy gossip was oblivious of these indignities heaped on me. I was too proud to cry or complain instead, I kept close to Moina and the frogs to avoid these brutes.

Not only were children brought to this broad patch of road for their outings but also dogs by their handlers. The pedigreed breeds were just as odd looking as the *babas*. They did not resemble any normal dog that I had seen. Some had short flat snouts, wiry fur; others were long but so short that their bellies almost touched the ground. Fat, white round ones which looked very much like the *babas* but displayed angry, red eyes and sharp vicious teeth, ready to dissect anyone if freed from their leashes. There was one, as tall and docile as a calf with an enormous head. The *babas*, took turns to ride on its back but I was too scared to do so, in case the dog sensed that I was not one of the regulars and swallowed me up whole.

I was always relieved when the sun went down and Moina's evening sessions came to an end. The frogs hurriedly gathered up their wards and made for home. For me, the steep hike back to Kanchanjungha *kothi* was like climbing mountain peak Kanchanjunga. I would beg Moina to carry me but no, she would drag me, pulling at my arm until it threatened to part company with its socket.

Once back home from our outing, Moina got busy with her duties but if ma was distracted, she would quietly make her way to the kitchen which was outside the flat. Her frequent visits to the kitchen were not to eat but to talk to Suren, our young cook.

Ma had appointed a young lad called Bahadur, he became my best friend and confidant. Kept me company and played with me, thereby saving me from coming in constant touch with Moina. This suited her fine as she could spend more time with Suren and less with me. Bahadur was aware of her friendship with the cook and disliked her for it.

At last we moved into our spanking new beautiful house, Monjula. This was a paradise for me. There were enough places for me to play. Oh, the joy of running around in my bare feet on the soft green grass, kept me busy all day.

Every day at 11 o'clock, Moina would come and pry me off my wanderings for a much needed bath. Bath times I disliked as she would drag me off unceremoniously, undress me, shove me into the bathroom and pour mugs of hot water on my head to wash off all the mud and dirt I had picked up all morning.

Things came to a head when, one morning, she dragged me away from an interesting game I was playing and started pulling off my clothes for bath. I rebelled, hitting her with my little hands and scratched her face. She slapped me hard on my cheek, back and legs. I had no option left but to sink my small milk teeth into her arm that held me tightly. She screamed, momentarily her grip relaxed, I broke away and shot under the low divan to protect myself from her vicious onslaught. I was out of her reach. She couldn't get under the divan. Unable to reach me, she found a long stick with which she started poking and whipping me.

Mad with pain and anger, I screamed and cried but there was nobody to hear me. Ma had gone shopping to the haat.

Bahadur and Suren were downstairs too far away to hear me. I had no weapons left, so I restored to verbal abuse, "You *randee,*" I screamed. It had the most dramatic effect on her. Her dark face peering at me, turned purple, her eyes bulged with shock and horror. She dropped the stick and ran howling to her favourite room, the kitchen.

I sat sobbing at the top of the stairs until ma arrived. As soon as Moina saw ma, the sweet, gentle Madonna started screaming like a banshee. Her head uncovered, long hair flying in all directions with blood shot eyes, pouring out gallons of tears, she told ma that she was leaving at once.

Ma shocked at Madonna's transformation, stared at her flabbergasted. "What is the matter Moina?" she asked concerned and utterly mystified. "Khuku, Khuku," she kept repeating. "What about Khuku?" ma asked alarmed. Then ma spotted me at the top of the stairs and her alarm turned to relief. "Khuku is a *saitan* she called me a *randee,"* Moina blurted out between her sobs. "I am leaving just now."

Ma tried to pacify Moina by putting her arms around her saying, "Khuku doesn't even know the meaning of that word, Moina. Why are you taking offence, she is only a little child." "Of course she knows what it means, just ask her?." "I know it is a bad word and she shouldn't have used it, she hasn't the slightest clue of its meaning. So don't take it to heart. Please, please forgive her. I will punish her for using such a bad word."

Ma was so agitated about Moina's leaving that she never found out what had made me use the word *randee.* I had picked up the word from Bahadur who had used it once, in disgust, to refer to Moina. It had not made any sense to me but I had remembered it and used it with amazing effect, to annihilate my torturous enemy for good.

Moina was adamant to leave for Calcutta so ma packed her off the next day. She could not be replaced so I spent my childhood happily in Bahadur's company at Monjula.

We went to Kolkata in winter with Suren in tow. Ma made inquiries about Moina and found her living in a miserable little room in a *bustee,* heavily pregnant. Ma pried it out of her that Suren was the father. My trusting ma had never suspected the affair between Moina and Suren. Now it dawned on ma why the word *randee* had hurt Moina to the core.

Ma insisted that Suren should marry her at once. Suren had no such intension but baba forced them to go to Kalighat, and get married. I had no idea of what was taking place. I found two wedding garlands hanging in the kitchen. I clapped my hands and exclaimed, "Moina and Suren are married!" I don't know how I came to such a conclusion but I was right. Suren disappeared soon after from our house and Moina's life for good.

A sweet little girl was born to Moina. We went to visit her with clothes and money. Moina, a Christian, couldn't go back to her family and Suren the bounder, had left her high and dry. We lost track of her after some time.

Many years later, Moina appeared at our Calcutta house. I was a mother now and just given birth to my first born. Ma and I did not recognize her until she told us her name. We were shocked at her appearance. Her long, black, tresses were gone, short wispy, untidy hair covered her head. a coarse cheap saree, was wrapped around her fat body, well above her ankles. The heels of her bare feet were badly cracked. Her bloated face with pan stained lips and corroded black teeth had completely replaced the serene, lissome beautiful Madonna of yester years forever.

Skeletons

Every morning, ma visited the site where our house was going to be built. I in my white *shola topee,* riding on Bahadur's back would follow her. Standing on the highest point we would look down to see the progress the coolies were making. Bands of coolies, men, women and children toiled all day landscaping, shaving the hill sides. Digging, flattening and filling the enormous crater in the center.

One day we noticed the coolies standing in a circle watching the others digging deep and pulling out bones. When we reached the circle of coolies, we found them standing around a heap of bones with grim faces, while the women and children looked terrified.

They were bones from skeletons, yellow with age. Bones, bones, bones from every part of the human body. Smooth round skulls with three black holes, protruding large teeth, stared straight at me, through their sightless sockets, sending jitters down my spine. I buried my face in Bahadur's back and screamed in terror.

Ma was just as terrified and ordered Bahadur to take me away from the ghastly scene at once. Just leaving the scene did not take away those horrifying images from my mind. Every time I closed my eyes, those skulls kept popping up in front of them, staring with their dark deep holes, teeth gnashing or opening in wide mirthless, raucous, deafening laughter. Mercifully the deep, sweet, carefree slumber of childhood obliterated those images until they reappeared with renewed vigour, in the middle of the night, making me scream and wet my bed.

It was discovered that our building site had been a burial ground long ago for the villagers. When the British arrived and started building their stone houses, they discovered solid rock strata at one end of the land. It became a stone quarry until it was exhausted, leaving an enormous crater.

The huge crater a deep hole with steep hillside around it did not discourage baba from buying it. In fact he found it a most challenging venture to convert this useless piece of land into a thing of beauty. This he did by landscaping it with great imagination and ingenuity.

Next morning was *haat* day so ma had to go shopping. Ma strictly forbade Bahadur, before she left, not to go to the building site with me till the bones were disposed off. Bahadur had other ideas. He persuaded me, that the skeletons were absolutely harmless. He would not only prove that to me but actually get me to lose all fear of them.

"Khuku, those ugly skulls can't harm us as they are of people dead long ago. Look at my face, if I lose all my flesh, eyes and nose, I will look like that too. We are all walking skeletons so don't be afraid, let's go down. I will show you how to put a whole skeleton together to make up a person. It will be like a jigsaw puzzle." I felt squeamish, still a bit afraid but didn't want to dampen Bahadur's enthusiasm and agreed to accompany him. My cousin Bishnu was visiting us for a few days after his graduation. He was eager to accompany us.

We trooped down the *chorbato,* me in my *shola topee,* on Bahadur's back with Bishnu bringing up the rear. When we reached the building site we found the *coolies* sitting glumly huddled together refusing to work. Illiterate, steeped in superstition, they did not want to disturb any more graves of their ancestors, expecting dire consequences and curses to descend on them.

Lulu *Babu,* the wily contractor, was telling them that these skeletons couldn't possibly belong to their ancestors. "They are hundreds of years old, of the Lephas who lived here, while you have come to live here recently. We will rebury these skeletons in a suitable place with due respect so that they lie in peace and their spirits will not disturb you. Moreover, there is no other house of this size being built in Kalimpong. So you will lose your jobs if you do not work here and your families will starve." The bottom line did the trick. The *coolies* reluctantly got up and started work, resigning themselves to their fate.

Bahadur raced down to the piles of bones as if he had discovered a cache of buried treasure. Bishnu followed just as eagerly only to draw back in horror as his eyes descended on those skulls, staring directly at him, through their sightless, deep, dark, sockets. Large splayed out, broken, discolored teeth ready to bite his head off.

Bahadur was highly amused by Bishnu's reaction. "Why *Babu,* you are not afraid of these lifeless skulls are you?" smiling, he picked up the biggest and most terrifying one with all its teeth bared in a leering grin and held it in front of Bishnu. He stepped back and begged Bahadur to drop it. He dropped me from his back instead and held the skull in front of me, took my little hand and put it on the smooth cranium gently. "Khuku, feel how smooth it is. Just like the boiled egg you have every morning for breakfast." To start with I felt queasy but soon the cool smoothness felt good as I rubbed my hand on it, my fear of the monstrous object started to fade away.

Bahadur never missed an opportunity to show off. He now hoisted up the skull in his hand, "Look at this specimen *Babu,* once he was a strong man like you. He has got a perfect set of teeth still intact. I wonder how he died so young. Come hold him *Babu.*" Bishnu was nervous; his fingers trembled and hesitated to touch the skull.

"Come, come, *Babu,* touch him, he is not going to bite you with his perfect set of teeth. He is dead. He can't harm anybody but you are afraid aren't you?"

"No, no. I am not at all afraid, give it to me," Bishnu said with a forced, weak smile, trying to put on a brave face as he held the skull gingerly.

"Come on *Babu,* feel the smoothness of his head, even Khuku felt it," Bahadur jeered. Bishnu made a show of running his fingers on the skull, then dropped it like a hot potato. Bahadur watching him keenly burst out laughing. "*Chi, chi Babu,* what a coward you are and you say you want to be a doctor, ha! ha! ha!"

The *coolies* had now gathered around us to watch the fun. They burst out laughing seeing Bishnu's discomfort and listening to Bahadur's barbs. Bishnu had to suppress his cowardice and salvage his pride.

"Who said I am afraid of these lifeless bones?" he shouted, picked up the skull and flung it as far as possible, like a shot put, ran up to the pile of bones and started kicking them vigorously, viciously.

Bahadur was not impressed by Bishnu's temper tantrum. "*Babu,* it is very fine kicking the skeletons in broad day light but can you do it at night?"

"Yes, why not," he cried on a sudden impulse puffing out his chest. A decision he would regret. "In that case *Babu,* will you come here all by yourself at midnight, pick up a bone to prove you were here and go back home?"

"Of course, why not, there is nothing to it." "Well then *Babu,* let's take a bet of ten rupees." "Done," said Bishnu at the spur of the moment.

That night we went to bed early as usual. I was suddenly woken up by loud noises coming from the dining room. I found myself alone in the dark without ma beside me. I ran out. I stood stock still at the dining room door surveying the scene before me dumbfounded.

Ma, Suren and Moina were desperately clutching a shivering, shuddering Bishnu trying to subdue his uncontrollable rigor. His terrified eyes were wide open staring blankly at the wall opposite. His chest heaved as he sucked in great gulps of air and let out a shrill, "*Ma go! Ma go*!" at regular intervals through parched lips and violently chattering teeth.

"Moina get some water, Suren get a hot water bottle," ma ordered in panic. Bishnu's well polished shoes were caked with mud. His shirt tails hung out of his dust laden pants. His neatly combed brilliantine hair now dusty and disheveled seemed to stand on end. His face was bereft of all colour.

Moina appeared with a whole jug of water and glass. Ma coaxed Bishnu to take a sip but he just couldn't put his mouth to the glass. So ma unceremoniously emptied the whole jug on his head. The cold water made him shiver even more. Suren appeared with the hot water bottle. "Stick it under his feet." ma yelled. All these procedures had no effect on Bishnu. He was in a state of deep shock and couldn't control his quivering body.

At this juncture Bahadur appeared and rubbing sleep out of his eyes, he surveyed Bishnu curiously. After much contemplation declared, "Ma, *Babu,* has got the fits." He yanked off ma's leather slippers, almost dislodging her. He stuck one under Bishnu's nose, the other between his chattering teeth. The chattering stopped as he gagged but his eyes still stared blankly. Bahadur's remedy had failed too. He turned to ma and said, "The only way is to put him to sleep." There were no tranquilizers available in those days but Bahadur had the perfect recipe.

He returned with a log wrapped in a *jharan* and before anyone could fathom his intention he gave Bishnu a resounding whack on the back of his head. Bishnu was out for the count. Bahadur jubilantly looked at the horrified faces all around him and put Bishnu to bed. Next morning Bishnu woke up, pale and drawn, nursing a sore head but back to normal to ma's great relief.

"Where did you go last night Bishnu?" ma asked, determined to get to the bottom of his strange behavior. Bishnu hesitated, looked sheepish but decided to come clean. "Last night, I went down to the building site." "But why?" asked ma mystified. "Well, I had taken a bet with Bahadur to prove that I was not afraid of the skeletons at the site and I would bring a bone back to prove it."

"I slipped out after everybody was asleep at midnight and found my way easily as it was a bright and beautiful moonlit night. I picked up a bone from the pile and was making my way up the slope when I heard a rattling behind me. I turned around and there in the shadows stood a skeleton. I couldn't believe my eyes; I stood rooted to the ground. *Kakima,* believe me, there was this monstrous skeleton standing upright, arms wide, skull nodding, teeth chattering staring straight at me through its dark sockets. All my self preservation instincts urged me to flee from this devil before it got me. My legs refused to carry me but I managed to climb up on all fours with the skeleton rattling behind me and I can still hear it. Once on top I ran all the way home and collapsed on the chair. I can't remember the rest."

He was now panting again and his terrifying experience sent several shudders down his spine. He clamped his hands over his face, started crying like a baby. Ma was flabbergasted. She didn't know whether to scold him or console him for his absurd story. She decided to do the latter in case he had another seizure. She wanted to avoid a repeat performance of the night before.

When Bishnu was alone, Bahadur ambled up to him with a wry smile. "Well, *Babu,* where is the bone?" Bishnu looked away embarrassed. "Can I have my ten rupees then Babu?" Bishnu to save himself more embarrassment and humiliation quickly handed him the money.

On our usual outing I asked Bahadur why he had lied to me about skeletons being lifeless. One had come alive and driven the daylights out of Bishnu. Bahadur laughed out loud, and then told me his story.

To make doubly sure to win his ten rupees, he had hurried down to the site in the evening, constructed a bamboo frame and strung up the bones to make a complete skeleton and ran back home. The skeleton hanging loosely, had turned into a wind chime, having more than the desired effect on poor Bishnu. Bahadur had gone down again, early in the morning, to dismantle the skeleton so that nobody could ever find out the master mind behind this diabolical plot, that had almost killed Bishnu and made him the laughing stock of Kanchanjungha *Kothi.* Bishnu cut short his holiday and left for Calcutta next day.

Hounds of Hell

Bahadur and I had scoured the whole of *Chibbo Basti* and Durbin Dara area. We had inspected every house from close quarters, sat in the gardens and taken shelter from rain in the verandah of the empty ones. There were no fencing, walls or gates to hinder us. Each property ran into the next with a line of trees or a hedge for demarcation. *Chors,* squatters, land, grabbers were non-existent. People of Kalimpong lived blissfully in peace.

The only house we had not dared to visit was *Topoban.* The residence of the Burma Raja and his family. We had heard tales of the Raja's violent temper and skills with the gun. At a party, in his house, he had flown into a right royal temper and slapped our dear *Phupu,* simply because she had asked him why he had adopted the local *mali's* son instead of a Burmese child.

The Raja was very fond of going on *shikar* and once on such an expedition, a young lad had been shot dead. Fortunately, not by him but by his friend Mr. Talukdar, a high up official in the British Government who had accompanied him. The young lad, a drummer boy, clad in a brown shirt, was mistaken for a deer by Mr. Talukdar who had shot him. All these stories and more made us give *Tapoban,* a wide berth.

Topoban is situated well below Upper Cart Road, completely hidden from the road by a high mound. A narrow gap in the mound, without a gate led to a long, narrow, winding drive to the house. To get a glimpse of the whole property, one had to go down the drive, a fair distance. Bahadur was determined to take a peek at the Raja's kingdom.

Throwing caution to the wind, one crisp and bright summer morning, he crept down the drive with me on his back. He stealthily made his way far enough to get a good view of the house and garden.

An immaculate garden met our eyes. An emerald green, manicured lawn, hemmed by wide beds of colourful and rare blossoms, were being tended by two industrious *malis*. Below the lawn was a clay tennis court. In one corner stood a grey double storied building with a red roof. Behind the house was a cow shed and a stable. We were fascinated by the Raja's residence which spelt decadent living.

Since nobody was around, only the *malis,* with their back turned towards us, Bahadur grew bolder and inched further down. Suddenly out of nowhere, two tall, grey dogs appeared. They stood on thin spindly legs with caved in stomachs. They pricked up their ears and sniffed the air, their mean round eyes focused on us. Bounding and leaping gracefully over the flower beds, they charged straight at us. I felt Bahadur going taut as he froze for a split second, then turned and desperately sprinted up the steep slope with a sudden spurt of energy.

I looked over my shoulder in utter panic. The dogs were barking furiously and coming straight for us at full speed. Snapping and snarling, their fangs bared, with red tongues and fierce amber eyes glittering. I screamed in terror. My white *shola topee* flew off my head and landed in front of the galloping dogs. I expected them to tear it to pieces but they paid no heed to it. They were not interested in any inanimate object when they had a fleeing prey to catch.

I dug my heels into Bahadur's rib cage to spur him on but his two short, sturdy legs were no match for the four thin ones. The hounds of hell fell on us like a flash of lightning. One of the dogs sunk his long, white, razor sharp teeth into

Bhadur's calf. He screamed in pain and keeled over. I clung on to him desperately terrified that the dogs would now bite a chunk of my bottom!

The dogs having landed their prey successfully, sat on their haunches guarding us. Their red, long tongues lolling out of their mouths, eyes glued on us, making sure we didn't escape from their clutches. Blood poured out of the deep holes in Bahadur's calf, dripping on the green grass forming a red pool. The *malis* had jumped into action as soon as they heard the dogs barking, streaking past them and my terrified screams. They arrived at last to rescue us.

One *mali,* caught the dogs by their collars and led them away while the other helped Bahadur to his feet and asked him to go to the house for first aid. Bahadur had clamped his hand on the wound to stop the bleeding but his red blood still oozed out through his stubby fingers. His face writhed in pain. I was sick with worry and started crying not knowing how to take away his pain or console him.

He refused to go into the house for first aid he would rather face the blood thirsty grey hounds than the unpredictable, ill tempered Raja. He would surely shoot us or slap us, for trespassing rather than reprimand or punish his well trained, ferocious, pampered dogs, which were only doing their duty. After much persuasion by the *mali,* Bahadur agreed to have his wound bandaged as the bleeding continued unabated.

I clutched Bahadur's hand tightly as he limped up to the verandah of the Raja's house and sat down. Suddenly the main door flew open and a short little man with a bushy moustache and eyebrows, wearing a short jacket above a checked silk *lungi,* black sandals, a funny turban tied in a knot on his head, an enormous *cheroot* stuck in his mouth, stepped out.

He gravely inspected Bahadur's wound and started barking out orders in short bursts of broken Hindi to the servants. "Fetch Dettol, iodine, water, cotton wool and bandage." He stood and watched, puffing at his *cheroot* as the servants got busy cleaning and bandaging Bahadur's wound properly. I tried to hide behind Bahadur's back as well as I could to avoid the eyes of this funny little man dressed so oddly. He was too busy conducting the dressing of the wound to notice me cringing and peeping at him from behind Bahadur's back.

Bandaging over to his satisfaction, the little man's face relaxed into a smile. Bahadur stood up with his head hanging over his chest, worried about what would come next. The little man patted Bahadur on one shoulder then the next as if knighting him. He then dug into his jacket pocket and fished out a crisp, brand new ten rupee note and slid it into Bahadur's shirt pocket. "Next time be careful," he said. The words barely audible through the profuse growth of hair on his upper lip and obstruction of the *cheroot*. Bahadur's eyes lit up. "*Salaam Sahib*," he uttered in delight.

As we walked home, I asked Bahadur, in amazement "Was the funny little man the Raja?" "Yes." "Well he is not at all terrifying but his dogs are." Bahadur was now walking on air, all his discomfort and pain forgotten. "I don't mind being bitten by those dogs every day, as long as the Raja keeps doling out ten rupee notes to me," he chuckled.

Many years later when I was a teenager, the Raja rented a house next to ours. He had lost all his wealth and his fair weather friends but not his pride. He took a great interest in me as I had picked up the two sports he loved best, tennis and shooting. We became good friends.

Putali Sahib

Phupu, was the first person in Kalimpong to start the flat system. Kanchanjungha *Kothi,* consisting of many rooms and out houses lay vacant so she decided to rent them out to people who can to live in Kalimpong, for an extended stay, or on a transferable job. It was not possible for them to rent a whole big house, nor was it possible to find one as absentee landlords did not believe in renting their premises.

Various people came to live in Kanchanjungha *Kothi* and formed one big happy family. The only family who did not mix with the others was an Anglo Indian family of four. Father, mother and two boys. They kept to themselves and the boys of five and seven never came to play in the yard with us children, perhaps, because they considered themselves superior to us, the natives. After all, they were fair skinned like our British rulers; their mode of dress and their life style were closer to theirs than ours.

The father, a young man, with a bullet head and crew cut was well tanned, slim and wiry. Every morning, I would see him going off in his half sleeved shirt, half pants with a butterfly net and bag. He didn't have a job. His only job was to go down to the Teesta River, every day, to catch *putalis.* He came back every evening, hot, tired and a few shades darker. There was a profusion of gorgeous *putalis* at the Teesta then. In October they made their way up to Kalimpong and adorned our gardens with their myriad hues. Now there are hardly any to enchant us.

This young man was referred to as the *Putali* sahib, being white and whose only occupation was catching butterflies and since nobody knew his name. His two sons dressed like him and looked like him, two miniature *Putali* sahibs.

Once in a while, I would see their mother's face, framed at the upstairs window, of their wooden house, that stood part from the main building where we lived. A round face with plump cheeks and wispy brown hair. She always looked sad and tired. I heard the servants whispering that she was heavily pregnant. Not knowing what pregnant meant, I assumed she had some kind of an infectious disease.

The two boys came down to play in the front garden sometimes. They looked colourless and skinny. They never had any visitors; they lived in their own ivory tower.

The *Putali* sahib's trips to the Teesta seemed to peter off. He spent most of his time at home with his two stuck up sons and invisible wife.

One night, everyone at Kanchanjungha *Kothi* was woken up by a huge commotion in *Putali* sahib's house. Sounds of flying pots, pans, shattering crockery followed by loud swearing flowed out of the open window to disturb us all. Everyone silently gathered on the court yard below the lighted windows. It was curiosity that drove them to listen to what was going on in the flat which usually was silent as a tomb. It was obvious that the husband and wife were having a quarrel. No one wanted to enter the war zone or interfere in their private warfare.

Suddenly a heavy cast iron, flying saucer like, frying pan, came flying out of the window missing Khaisa *daju 's* woolly hair by inches. A ripple of suppressed laughter went through the crowd. I too burst out laughing at our window from where

I was watching all the fun. Ma was pacing the court yard wringing her hands, extremely perturbed. She didn't know how to help or save the poor pregnant woman from her husband's insane wrath. *Phupu,* just as worried as ma was slowly making her way down stairs to the court yard.

More shouts, scream interrupted by thumps, whacks, could be heard until, shrill piercing screams rent the air, *Phupu,* could stand it no longer. She thumped up the wooden stairs of *Putali* sahib's house as fast as her portly proportions would allow, followed by ma and me. She banged on the door. At last there was pin drop silence inside. The door opened to a crack, bright light sliced the darkness. "Open the door at once," yelled *Phupu.* The crack grew larger and the bullet head of *Putali* sahib appeared. Without waiting for an invitation, *Phupu,* gave the door a resounding kick. It flew open.

We were shocked to see the state of the battle ground. "This room is reeking of alcohol" *Phupu* pronounced puckering up her small nose. "So you have been drinking Mister don't light a match, we will all be blown up," she declared.

The room looked like a disaster zone with broken crockery lying on the wooden floor. Dented pots and pans lay everywhere minus the heavy frying pan, which had flown out of the window, a deadly missile which could have carried *Putali* memsahib's head on it, ready for frying, if it had only been aimed more carefully. But *Putali* sahib's unsteady hands had saved him from the gallows.

The two little boys huddled in the safest corner clinging to each other, too petrified to cry. Their mother lay flat on the floor groaning, her enormous stomach heaving with each laboured breath. Angry red welts covered her bare legs, arms and face. *Phupu,* lifted her head gently and helped her to sit up, wiping the blood that dripped from her nose. Both her eyes were hardly visible through the swollen, blue black eyelids. *Phupu,* cradled her in her arms soothing her battered body and ravaged soul.

Ma attended to the children, coaxing them to go to bed, patting them to a fitful slumber, full of terrifying nightmares that would haunt them all their lives.

Putali sahib sat on the floor, his thin legs protruding from his baggy half pants, supporting his bullet head with his large red hands. He didn't dare to look up and meet the two pairs of accusing eyes focused on him. He was indeed the culprit of the mayhem.

For the first time in my life I saw ma losing her temper. She addressed *Putali* sahib in a fury, "How dare you beat your wife? A strong sturdy man like you, beating a woman, that too pregnant with your child? You call yourself a man, you have no shame you despicable worm? You take your frustration out on a helpless woman in your drunken state. Why don't you vent your anger on somebody your own size?"

Phupu, was prompting ma in Hindi. "Yes, yes, tell him that next time he wants to pick on a helpless woman to try me." The vision of such an encounter sent a visible shudder up *Putali* sahib's rather weak spine. He sobered up somewhat and fell at *Phupu,*'s feet and begged for mercy. "Don't fall at my feet, fall at your wife's feet and beg for mercy. Next time you behave like this, I shall call the police and throw you out of my house." *Phupu,* bellowed. She knew that the man's punishment would be great if only he had a British employer to sort him out.

Next morning *Putali* memsahib delivered a girl, a beautiful baby, *Putali.*

Ma

At this point of time, ma devastated by my sister's untimely death, kept to herself. She had lost interest in life, even me. She just carried on with her parental duties in a detached manner. I could not awaken any spontaneous love, affection or companionship in her for me. She lived in a world of her own. A world of sorrow and depression.

Her large eyes and beautiful face never lit up with a smile. Her constant mournful long sighs rose from the very depth of her troubled soul. Tears came out of my eyes only when I had a good reason to cry but ma's tears rolled down her cheeks often without rhyme or reason. I would stare at the droplets in amazement, suddenly aware, that I was staring at her, she would quickly wipe them away with the *achal.*

I was put completely in charge of my ayah, Moina. It was her duty to take care of all my needs which she performed mechanically. To her relief and my enjoyment, ma engaged a small *tattu,* to take me for a ride every morning. The *tattu,* belonged to John Macdonald who lived on the plot of land where Chomiomo, stands today. Having left the army he was enjoying life with his Nepali wife and children in a small white washed house with a red roof. He owned a few ponies which were in great demand by the British children of our area.

Ma had chosen the small *tattu,* for me as I was too small to ride the ponies. The *tattu,* had a special saddle with a ring around it to stop me from falling off. Every morning the *sais,* would arrive with the *tattu* in tow. I would be made ready in my riding breeches and a white *shola topee,* for my daily ride which I loved. I couldn't handle the reins so I hung on to the saddle ring while the *sais,* led the *tattu.* I would be fast asleep on the saddle by the time I arrived home.

Hoisted out of my rocking seat, I would open my eyes to see ma bathed and ready in a wide bordered white *saree,* drying her long black hair in the sun. "Moina give Khuku a bath immediately, she is smelling of the *tattu.*" I hated these bath times given by Moina. Dettol baths were essential to kill off all germs, specially T.B. Germs, real or imaginary.

Moina would rush me through the ritual as fast as possible without giving me a chance to play with water which I longed to do. I lived in a protective sanitized bubble. The house reeked of carbolic soap and Dettol even though the doors and windows were kept wide open to let in as much fresh air and sunlight as possible. All clothes back from the *dhobi,* were sunned and I was not allowed to handle any coins as they were handled by beggars therefore store house of germs. It was T.B Germs that had killed her beloved daughter so now she was paranoid about germs.

If bathing was a painful exercise, mealtimes were more so. I was a poor eater so ma would sit opposite me at the table and construct little balls of well mashed rice *dal,* and vegetables with her fingers on my silver *thali.* Each ball represented a person I knew, she would then pop each ball in to my reluctant mouth to chew and swallow. These balls were far more insipid than the people they represented. I would spend hours trying to push them down my gullet. This being the age old method of feeding children by their mothers. Ma knew, if left to my devices, I would not eat enough to sustain myself and my fingers were never clean.

Bed time was the best time of all. I would cuddle up to her in bed feeling her warmth course through me. I would cling to her as tightly as possible so that she couldn't escape but she invariably did. As soon as sleep turned my tired body in to putty, she would extricate herself from my now limp octopus grip and sit at a small table, under a dim light. Often disturbed by a nightmare I would wake up with a start, to find her writing in her diary. This she did every night, sometime till dawn. I would beg her to join me in bed to comfort me and to lull me back to sleep again. This she did reluctantly.

Many years later I came across a pile of ma's diaries filled with a running commentary, informing my dead sister of day to day happenings at Kanchanjungha *Kothi* and my escapades in great detail and how much she missed her every moment of the day.

Now I realize the therapeutic value of writing. She poured out all her innermost feelings into those diaries, night after night for years. Thoughts and feelings she couldn't tell or share with anybody. Pouring her heart out must have brought some relief to her highly emotional state of mind. Nobody would have had the patience to listen to her sorrow or found words to console her. Her outpouring of grief on paper was the best healer.

Phupu, realizing ma's state of mind kept her company as often as possible. She was like a mother to her, giving her every possible advice she could to sooth her troubled mind but ma was inconsolable. Her sorrow knew no bounds. In fact she grieved for her beloved Bula all her life. She gave up entirely my sister's favourite fare. She never touched them ever.

She would observe her birthdays and death anniversaries every year. She would decorate dozens of her photos with garlands and the choicest flowers from her garden and light incense sticks. She would invite people to come and sing those sad *Rabindra sangeet,* all related to death. On those days only boiled vegetarian food was cooked as it was a day of mourning. All day ma was sad and unapproachable.

Phupu was very happy when ma decided to do something for the women of Kalimpong. She was always interested in the upliftment of women. She maintained that there was more to a woman's life than being tied to the kitchen sink, reduced to a life of drudgery and slavery. Of course husband and children came first, then what?

Usually her spare time is wasted in gossip when she can use it to improve herself, acquire knowledge not for her benefit only but to bring up her children better. To become self-sufficient. It is degrading to ask husbands for a little money for fulfilling every little desire or frivolity. So why not earn a little pocket money by learning a useful trade to meet her aspiration and fancies or an egg nest for a rainy day?

With this end in view ma borrowed a room in the centre of Kalimpong town. That room is now Misra medicine store.

She invited ladies to come and learn knitting, sewing, tailoring, making pickles, jam, jellies etc. Apart from all this she would teach them about health and hygiene, rearing of children, discuss family issues, give them world news and read stories to them.

All this she did by missing her beauty sleep every afternoon and walking to the town to improve the lot of the women, to enlighten them so that they could hold their heads up high and become productive, confident, individuals.

After a few months of selfless hard work, put in by ma, the activities in the small room, in town, came to a grinding halt. The women preferred gossip to enlightenment!

Not to be daunted by this failure, ma concentrated on the children. She opened a club for them and called it Monimala. The children came in hordes to spend their Sundays with *Mashima,* since they had neither television nor any other type of entertainment. Ma involved them in dancing, singing, acting, drawing, painting, recitation. Read stories to them, took them for picnics. She encouraged them to act in short plays which were staged in Kalimpong town and much appreciated by the public.

She was far more successful with the children than with the adults. Ma loved being with them as much as they loved being with her. I hated these kids as they got her full attention while I didn't.

Ma's solace came when our house was being built. Every morning she would go to the building site to supervise the work as baba was away in Calcutta. This daily routine made her forget her sorrow for a few hours. It took many years for her to lead a normal life even though my sister's memory haunted her forever.

In later years ma became quite a socialite and took on *Phupu's* mantle as the first lady of Kalimpong once *Phupu,* passed away.

Monjula

Baba had bought a plot of land in the new Development area of Kalimpong which was far from developed. It was a vast steep hillside full of shrubs, encircled by Upper Cart Road and Lower Bridle Road. The proposed Atisha Road, to serve this area, was only on paper yet, a few Bengalis had built houses on this desolate area. The building plots of different sizes and categories were leased to each buyer for a period of 99 years. The buyers happily bought them as no one expected to live out the lease period.

The British had already bought large tracts of land and built their summer houses on the top of the mountain with the best view of Kanchanjungha. The new comers had no choice but to buy whatever land was available to them in the Development area.

One day baba, very proudly, took ma and me, on Bahadur's back, to see the land. Ma's enthusiasm vanished as we stood on the over grown hillside that plunged steeply into a deep crater. To make matters worse, ma almost lost her balance as a jackal, disturbed by our intrusion, shot past her, nearly dropping her into the deep crater. "Where are we going to build a house, there is no flat land anywhere and it is infested with wild animals?" she wailed. Baba smiled and said, "Don't worry just wait and see." Ma's disappointment and gloom gave her a few days respite from her never ending grief, she had an added worry.

Baba appointed a local Nepali contractor called Lulubabu to start work on the land. Baba carefully and ingeniously prepared the landscaping of the hopeless plot of land and gave him blue prints to follow. He came up often from Calcutta to see the progress made. Ma was to go down every day to supervise. This gave her some purpose in her life.

Lulubabu started work with his ragged group of *coolies* comprising of men, women and children under the eagle eyes of a *Baider.* Soon the obstinate piece of land started taking shape. Bahadur would take me down to the site on his back sometimes. We would stand at the highest point and look down in wonder at the bands of *coolies* working below, cutting, shaping, digging, hewing, leveling, battling to convert the unwieldy, stubborn, inhospitable hillside and a huge crater to boot, habitable.

The activity below was akin to the MGM biblical movies depicting bands of slaves toiling to construct Pyramids in Egypt.

The huge crater in the middle of our land was not formed by a volcano but man made. It used to be a stone quarry as well as a burial ground. The stones had all been removed leaving a crater behind and bones of people long dead.

Young boys and girls worked at the site along with their parents in ragged clothes and bare feet. The young mothers brought their babies in bamboo cradles and left them in the shade. Most of the time they slept peacefully in spite of the noise and the swirling dust. If one whimpered or cried the mother would press him to her breast or shove a banana into his mouth to satisfy his hunger pangs and to keep him quiet.

The workers and coolies had their lunch at the little makeshift tea shop near the building site. These shops always sprung up near all building sites to serve tea, *puri* and *aludam.* Piping hot *Puris,* puffed and round, served on a leaf with red hot *aludam.* They looked delectable, far more appetizing than the insipid food I had to swallow every day.

Any food outside the house was strictly taboo for me. This fact both Bahadur and I were aware of. Whenever Bahadur had 1 *anna* he would buy six *puris* with a big dollop of *aludam,* eat them with great relish, smacking his lips as tears glistened in his eyes from the spicy red hot *aludam.* He would stick out his tongue and suck in great gulps of air to cool it.

One day I persuaded Bahadur to buy me a portion of this delectable snack. I didn't dare to touch the fiery *aludam,* so I stuffed a *puri* into my mouth. It was wonderful! I was about to eat the next one when ma appeared on the scene suddenly. "What are you eating?" she screamed. Her face horror stricken. With that she snatched the remaining *puris,* out of my hand and flung them on the ground. My heart sank and tears of sorrow flowed down my cheeks to see the delicious *puris* lying forlornly at my feet covered in dust.

Most of the workers brought their own lunch, they couldn't afford the *puris.* Their lunch consisted of roasted corn which were hard as pellets and cold black tea, laced with salt, as sugar was too expensive. Corn was their staple food.

The workers were paid handsomely, according to their expertise. The carpenters were paid Re 1.8 *annas* per day, masons Re 1.4 *annas,* male coolies 8 *annas,* women 4 *annas,* children 1 *anna.* If the whole family worked together every day, they made a considerable sum per week. Pay day was Friday, Saturday being *haat* day and a holiday. The men waited eagerly for pay day. They would drown themselves, that evening, in *rakshi.*

Jobs were scarce as very few houses were built in those days. People were extremely poor. The children wore hand me downs, worn threadbare. Nobody had shoes. They lived in mud houses with thatched roofs. Slept on the mud floor. Fetched water from the nearest spring. Bathing was a luxury and rarely indulged in.

Lulubabu was following baba's plans meticulously and lo and behold as if by magic, three large flat building sites appeared to ma's delight. The deep, bottomless crater had been filled enough to provide another flat piece of land. At a lower level, a large enough, Olympic size swimming pool complete with sunbathing area.

Baba was all set to build a swimming pool after the house was built but he gave up the idea when he calculated the cost of cement. It was then Re 1 per bag! I am glad that he gave up the idea as there is no water in Kalimpong anymore! The irony is that water diviners have detected a very large pool of water directly below the intended swimming pool recently.

Then a high mound was built, a hillock, a view point with a 360 degrees view of the mountains. The landscaping created by baba from a useless piece of land was a marvel, unparalleled in Kalimpong.

The house started taking shape and built in record time. Every piece of material for the building, except the stones and wood, came all the way from Calcutta to Siliguri then by rope way to Kalimpong. I remember seeing the rope way going down from a point in the 10th. Mile. It was an easy and cheap way of transporting goods, I don't know why it was discontinued. Today cable cars could have replaced it. The British had thought of everything for Kalimpong including a toy train from Siliguri to Galikhola near Teesta Bazar.

The dream house was completed at last. A stone house with wooden floors, several verandahs, large picture windows in every room for a panoramic view of the Kanchanjungha and its sister ranges, the ink blue mountains and valleys. Below each picture window was a wide divan where one could lie and watch the clouds floating towards the mountain peaks.

Baba had ordered so much building material that a garage was built at a lower level although, he had no intention of buying a car, walking was the only mode of travel in the hills he maintained. Baba was always building so eventually the garage turned into another house.

What to name the house was the next question? No name seemed suitable. Until I hit upon Monjula. I got the idea from the MacDonald's who had named their house Joyce Villa after, their daughter who had died so why not name our house after my dead sister? Although the property has changed hands now, people still know it as Monjula.

Once the house was completed ma's enthusiasm knew no bounds, she set about making a wonderful garden. She ordered exotic plants from a nursery in Rhenoc, planted and reared then with love and care. Two pergolas for creepers, flower beds filled with seasonal flowers, fruit trees and pines. She turned it into a paradise. This is where I spent my childhood. The most wonderful years of my life!

Monjula was ma's pride and joy, a fitting tribute to her beloved daughter. She loved it and so did I. It was the only place we called home where we lived the happiest years of our lives. Unfortunately Monjula was burnt down during the Gorkha agitation in 1988. It left me heartbroken forever but I am glad ma passed away before that happened.

As for baba, he would have been totally heartbroken too if he had lived, not only to see Monjula in ruins but to see his intricate and sublime landscaping completely submerged and obliterated by mounds of mud and made into one piece of flat land without any contours or character.

The house is gone, the land flattened but the name remains and will for years to come and the memories of my childhood paradise will never fade.

The Unsolved Mystery

In the early 1940s electric light had not reached the new Development area of Kalimpong. We happily used kerosene lamps and enjoyed the moonlit nights. We had no need for refrigerators or fans since the weather was several degrees cooler then.

Atisha Road had not been built but very much on the map. Without a road, the poles for bringing electric wires could not be fixed. There was no dire necessity to do so since there were only seven houses built along the proposed road at that time. This was the first road the British gave an Indian name to. It was named after Buddha's famous disciple Atisha Dipankar who had traveled all the way to Tibet years ago.

Life went on as usual in Monjula minus electricity. Guests came from Calcutta and enjoyed the candle lit dinners and rustic atmosphere.

Kalimpong was then a peaceful, quiet safe haven. So safe, that baba didn't even bother to fix a back door to our house. The passage from the back verandah led straight to a large landing of the stairs, the kitchen and pantry. All the bedrooms, dining and drawing rooms had flimsy glass doors. There was no question of fixing grills on picture windows to obstruct the view. There were no *Chors* or robbers. All doors and windows remained wide open throughout the day. Kalimpong was more than safe.

Baba's best friend Mr. Khagen Dasgupta, the owner of the well known Calcutta Chemical Company, the inventor and manufacture of the famous Mango soap and Neem toothpaste, was our house guest along with his wife.

It was monsoon time. Each night blinding rain came down in torrents drumming on the tin roof, obliterating all other sound. On such nights we had candle lit dinner and retired to bed early. Khagen Babu and his wife occupied the master bedroom upstairs next to the one in which baba, ma and I slept. Downstairs was quite empty except for Bahadur who slept there.

One night, we were woken up by frantic loud cries of "*Chor! chor!*" downstairs. Baba jumped out of bed, opened the bedroom door and rushed downstairs in his pajamas with ma trailing behind and me clinging to her fearfully. There was a no torch around and no time to light a candle.

At the foot of the stairs stood Bahadur, screaming "*Chor! chor*!" at the top of his voice. He looked shaken and petrified by the light of the flickering candle he held in his hand. Baba caught him by the shoulders and shook him, "Just stop shouting and go to bed, you have had a bad dream, now go to sleep like a good boy," baba said sternly.

"No, no, it is not a dream sahib, I saw him, I almost caught him."

"Where is he now?"

"He slipped out of my hands and fled through the pantry."
"Now please Bahadur, stop your nonsense and go back to bed, there are no *chors,* in Kalimpong you know that?"

Bahadur almost in tears now trying to convince baba that he had seen the *chor,* clearly, it was not a dream. Ma and I came down to sooth and calm the agitated Bahadur.

Now Khangenbabu descended, bleary eyed with sleep. "What is the matter?" he asked decidedly annoyed by the disturbance. "I am sorry for waking you up, Bahadur here, had a bad dream, he saw a *chor* in his dream," laughed baba.

Khagenbabu groggy with sleep all this time, suddenly woke up. "Where is the *chor*? what has he stolen?" he asked agitated wide awake now.

"No, no, there are no *chors* in Kalimpong. Nobody came, Bahadur is just imagining things, go back to sleep" said baba soothingly.

Satisfied, Khagenbabu, a big built, heavy man went shuffling up the stairs in his bedroom slippers. At the top of the stairs on the banisters he noticed his *Punjabi*, lying limply. He was sure he had taken it off before going to bed and hanging it carefully on the clothes horse in the bedroom. How did it come here? Surely his memory was not playing tricks.

Unable to figure out the transportation of the *Punjabi*, from the bedroom to the banisters, he picked it up, to put it back in its original place. He then remembered that he had kept two crisp notes of Rs. 100 in the book pocket of his *Punjabi*, yesterday. He quickly put his hand into the book pocket, wide awake now, searching for the notes, only to find the pocket empty.

He was so agitated by this discovery that he screamed, "*Chor! chor*!" Baba bounded up the stairs two at a time, ma, me and Bahadur followed as fast as we could.

"Where is the c*hor*?" baba demanded looking around.

"I don't know."

"Then why are you screaming like that?"

"My money is gone the *chor* must have taken it."

"Where did you keep it?" "In the usual place, my *Punjabi* pocket, see it is empty now."

"See, I told you there was a *chor* in the house," cried Bahadur jubilantly.

Baba was flabbergasted. "A *chor*, in Kalimpong, that too in my house, impossible, you must have mislaid the money, how much was it'?" "Two hundred rupees," cried Khagenbabu.

Khagenbabu's wife woken up last, by the agitated voices, rolled out of the bed room. "What is the matter *Ogo*?" she asked yawning. "Didn't I put two hundred rupee notes in my pocket yesterday or did you pick my pocket?" he asked her accusingly.

"Oh, dear, why should I pick your pocket?" "Only because you are in the habit of doing so."

Baba seeing the embarrassment on the lady's face and sensing a heated argument, between husband and wife, in the middle of the night, quickly changed the subject.

"Now, now, Khagenbabu, tell me where did you keep your *punjabi* with the money in it?"

"Why, in my bedroom and now it was hanging on the banister without the money."

"How did the *chor* get into your bedroom since the door was locked?"

"Well, I had left the door open since I was hot," Khajenbabu admitted sheepishly.

Bahadur, who was listening to this conversation intently now piped up. "There see, I told you there was a *chor* in the house, he obviously took the money, I saw him, now do you believe me, dreaming indeed," he flung at them smugly. Now there was no disbelieving him.

All this time I was following everybody around enjoying the suspense of the midnight adventure. Now that it was established that a *chor* had actually entered the house and stolen a large sum of money, I was terrified, in case he was still around, lurking in the shadows. I clung to ma tightly shaking with fear.

Bahadur saw me trembling with tears rolling down my face. "What is the matter Khuku, why are you crying?" He asked me kindly.

"The *chor* is still around and I am afraid of him," I sobbed. "Don't worry, I chased him away, he is gone, come with me everybody, I will show you how the *chor* got away." All of us trooped downstairs behind him.

Bahadur, my constant companion and best friend, was a great story teller. He would keep me enthralled for hours with stories that came alive with plenty of action thrown in. He was very fond of dramatics.

Now was his chance to show off his talent to an audience eager to solve the mystery of the missing money.

The stage was set. The dim lights from the lamps, flashes of bright lighting outside, the grim audience, watching him intently from the shadows, was the perfect setting.

Bahadur entered the dining room, closing the glass door behind him. This was his curtain. He then opened the door gently, the curtain was up, his eyes fixed on the big steel meat safe just in front. Now Bahadur's commentary with live actions unfolded.

"Now, watch me, I was fast asleep when I heard the metallic sound of this meat safe door. I woke up thinking; perhaps one of you, feeling hungry, had come down to raid the meat safe for a midnight snack. I didn't bother but the sound of the creaking door persisted so I got out of bed and looked out through this glass door. I couldn't believe my eyes. There was a big man, this big, in a raincoat and hat, bending down in front of this meat safe pointing a torch inside and helping himself to the food. I had no option but to grab him since, I had no weapon to hit him with," Bahadur crouched down, his arms wide open, eyes fixed in front and took a mighty leap in the air and landed on the now absent *chor.*

He fell on the floor rolling and grappling with the imaginary *chor* with a flood of choices epithets, groans and shouts. Then lay still and looked at the pantry through which the *chor* had run out extricating himself from Bahadur's grasp.

He got up and ran to the pantry window, "See, he broke this glass pane to enter the house. He kept the window wide open for a quick get away."We inspected the window in turn the pane was broken.

Everybody seemed quite satisfied with Bahadur's action packed story with enough proof. Khagenbabu still smarting from the loss of his Rs. 200, patted him on the back and said, "*Sabash.*" Ma and Mrs. Dasgupta heaped praise on him for his bravery. In my eyes he became a larger than life hero but baba still looked puzzled.

Thinking aloud he said, "Why did the thief go through so much trouble of smashing a window pane to come in, then fleeing through the same window when there is no back door? He could have sailed in and sailed out without any obstruction. *Chors* always find the easiest access."

Next day the police was informed. They arrived loaded with bags of paraphernalia. Everybody was questioned specially Bahadur about last night's occurrence. Bahadur was once again the chief actor, describing the midnight encounter with gusto, leaping in the air higher than ever to pounce on the unsuspecting *chor*, rolling on the ground trying to pin down the now absent *chor*.

The police man heard him out patiently not quite in the mood to enjoy his antics or award a bravery medal to him.

They checked the window and just below it, they found a foot print on the soft earth. It was the print of a shoe. This was the only clue they found. Very excited, they set about opening their heavy bags mixing a white powder with water. This turned into a viscous liquid which they poured into the deep shoe imprint. I watched all these proceedings with great interest.

After a long wait the police triumphantly took out a perfect solid white mould of the shoe print cast in plaster of Paris. This they carried away with assurances of catching the *chor* soon. I never figured out how they were going to achieve this impossible feat. We never heard from them again. They at least showed some interest and did their job to impress us. After all Rs. 200 was a small fortune then.

Baba immediately built a solid wooden door to shut off the back entrance and one on the staircase as well. Funnily enough, both these doors perished when Monjula was set on fire but the flimsy window of the pantry through which the thief was supposed to have exited still remains.

Years later, when I was old enough to think logically, discrepancies about the thief story struck me as very odd. The description of the *chor* didn't match anybody in Kalimpong of those days. It was only expected that if a poor fry came to steal he would be dressed in meager clothes not in a raincoat, hat, shoes and possess a torch. This *chor* belonged in the pages of a sophisticated English detective thriller.

Bahadur could neither read nor write, he was not in the habit of seeing English movies so, was the well dressed *chor* a figment of his fertile imagination? He used to leaf through English magazines, perhaps he had seen such a picture in one of them. Had he then carefully choreographed the whole episode, scripted, directed and enacted it with maximum effect and authenticity of the missing Rs 200, to win kudos, trust and unquestionable life-long gratitude of the Mitter family in one fell swoop?

I often wonder whether Bahadur was smart enough to have planned and executed the perfect crime to the last detail of planting the imprint of a shoe or had a thief actually come!

The King and I

Ma had taken to her bed sobbing in the darkened bedroom in the middle of the day. This was unusual and I was perturbed.

Later that night I discovered the cause of her sorrow. Baba had committed the most unforgivable crime. He had let out her beloved home Monjula, to a Chinese family for a year. He had just not been able to resist the generous offer of Rs. 200 per month.

Ma was inconsolable. How could he let out her beloved home to complete strangers? The house whose construction she had supervised with such love, care and enjoyed living in.

We shifted into the lower house. The Chinese family arrived with loads of luggage and settled into our home. There were just four of them. Mr. And Mrs. King, an old aunt and a man servant. I was surprised that Mr. King was not a king but a business man. What was even more surprising was that the young couple was slim, tall and very good looking, very unlike the Chinese people I was used to seeing in those days.

Mr. King had a long narrow face with delicate features. His eyes were not almond shaped. His jet black brilliantine hair parted down the middle, sat like raven's wings on either side his flat head. His smooth skin was tinged with yellow. He wore a very smart, perfectly tailored, light yellow suits which enhanced the pallor of his skin, making him look very much like me when I had jaundice.

He looked every inch a prosperous business man with his solid gold watch, cuff links, sober ties and highly polished brown shoes.

By contrast I thought his wife looked plain but certainly very attractive and tall to boot. Delicately rouged, lips ticked with a halo of permed hair, she dressed elegantly in pants and matching tops.

They made a very handsome couple. Devoted to each other. Unfortunately they had no children. He had rented Monjula to spare his delicate wife the heat and dust of Calcutta. Very soon Mr. King departed to attend to his business, leaving his forlorn wife behind. We didn't set eyes on her for three days. When she eventual appeared in the garden, her face and eyes bore marks of unabated tears.

Ma's heart went out to her at once. Her firm resolution to stay away from the strangers, usurpers of her beloved home, dissolved and faded into thin air. She walked up to Mrs. King, put her arms around her and gently steered her into our house for tea and sympathy.

Inside her sophisticated exterior lived a frightened, insecure child longing to be loved. She soon fell prey to ma's charms which lay in her simplicity and sincerity. She became absolutely devoted to ma and spent most of her time with her although, she had been provided with a chaperon, the elderly aunt.

She could barely speak a few words of English but picked up enough from ma to make herself understood, she never stepped out of Monjula. She didn't need to.

The lovelorn princess languished in the lap of luxury in the Garden of Eden, patiently waiting for the prince to come and rescue her, not from a tyrant or a witch but from boredom.

Ma was much impressed by the Chinese cook. Super efficient, he cooked, cleaned the bathrooms, the whole house, shopped and cooked the most delicious meals. While ma had a separate servant for each job.

Always dressed in a spotless white shirt and pant, he would go shopping on *haat* days so would ma. He would ride back home in a taxi while ma would come walking home with a over laden *coolie,* in tow, to save the exorbitant taxi fare of Rs. 2!

Ma was in awe of this cook. Baba jokingly asked her if she would like to have such a cook. She flatly refused. "He is a *laat saab,* his salary is more than all my servants put together, moreover, he sits at table with the family for all meals." baba was amused, "Don't you know the Chinese always eat at table with all their servants?" he asked.

Often I would creep into their kitchen through the back door just to watch him cook. I would watch fascinated as he chopped up vegetables at lightning speed, all his movements precise and quick. Deftly he would toss and turn food in the large *wok* and lo and behold the most mouth watering dishes would be cooked and turned out in minutes. It was sheer magic. He was the most proficient magician.

He was a very serious man. No hint of a smile ever crossed his lips and he didn't like anyone to invade the privacy of his kitchen, to steal his trade secrets, not even a mere child.

He completely ignored me. Undaunted by his indifference, I still persisted in going and standing by the door, until

I saw him cutting up a solid lump of congealed, dark red pig's blood into cubes for a certain dish. The cubes quivered and shook like jelly. I ran out feeling quite sick never to return.

One morning I persuaded ma to take me to visit Mrs. King. We walked into the sitting room to find the elderly aunt busy with a piece of embroidery. She was tiny. Seeing us she smiled displaying a set of enormous teeth, two of them golden. They were as large as Red Riding Hood's wolf grandmother's.

Mrs. King arrived but did not bother to introduce us to her as she spoke only Chinese, so she went back to her embroidery much relieved. Ma asked Mrs. King why aunt was never seen outside. "She is afraid the sun will ruin her white skin and make it brown, moreover she can't walk much." We both looked down at her feet. They were tinier than mine and looked deformed. Her feet were disproponate to her body.

Mrs. King explained that her aunt's feet had been tied, bound and encased in iron shoes since babyhood to stop them from growing. It was unladylike to have large feet. The ladies from rich families never had to do any work. They lived a life of leisure displaying their useless little feet to be admired. I thanked my lucky stars that I was not born in China.

Months later Mr. King arrived laden with gifts for his beloved but he hadn't forgotten me. He had brought me a small red rubber ball. I was thrilled.

Mr. King decided to throw a large dinner party for a few Chinese families of Kalimpong to meet his wife. He was keen that she should get to know them to give her company but she never got friendly with any of the families, except for one who owned Home Studio in the 10th mile. Their children visited Mrs. King often to my delight. Their latest edition, a baby girl, was adopted by the Kings.

These children attended the only Chinese school in town, in Bung Bustee, now Green hills. Mr. Shen was the head master. There were only four classes so when the children passed out they went to higher schools in town. The school put up very interesting magic shows and concerts to which ma and I were always invited.

The Chinese community was small but very well knit. Most of them were shoe makers, some well to do business men. Mr. David Macdonald had brought a group of Chinese to Kalimpong from China. They were the prisoners of the Tibetan army awaiting a gory end. Mr. Macdonald to save them from such a fate brought them with him to Kalimpong. These men settled down here and married local girls and passed themselves off as locals to avoid any further trouble. Their descendants still live here. Others left Kalimpong for good.

I was looking forward to the dinner. I was the only child invited. Bahadur, warned me that the Chinese ate each other's *jutha*. "Don't drink any wine," he said. "What is wine?" I asked. "It is a drink you get drunk on it." "What is drunk?" "Drunk, see this is being drunk," and the very next minute his shoulders slumped, his arms hung down loosely, his legs turned to jelly. He weaved around the room knocking into furniture. His eyes rolled, speech slurred. After a few tottering turns and wild lunges to steady himself, he landed in a heap near the door.

I ran to him shook his inert body and implored him to wake up but to no avail. I decided to call ma when he suddenly sat bolt upright. Normal again, he smiled at me. "Don't do this again," I cried, relieved. Bahadur was an excellent actor. He enacted every story that he told me making them come alive and holding me spell bound. This bit of acting I didn't find amusing.

Ma and I arrived at the party in good time as the Chinese eat early dinner. The long table was laid out with delicate Chinese bowls, plates and to my horror, a pair of ivory chop sticks. In the right hand corner stood the tiniest stemmed glass containing a brown liquid. This must be deadly wine that drove people out of their senses I surmised.

Mr. King stood up, picked up the tiny delicate glass, held it high to propose a toast to his beautiful wife. Everybody followed suit excepting me. Mr. King was waiting for me to hold up my glass. My arms had turned to led, I couldn't lift them. Ma standing beside, urged me too but I looked at her hopelessly. Visions of Bahadur's inebriated state boggling my mind.

With the greatest effort I lifted the glass. Mr. King proposed the toast, put the glass to his lips and knocked it back. Everybody followed suit. Ma put the glass to her lips and put it down. I too brought the glass up to my lips, suddenly a strong over powering smell shot up my nostrils, making me sneeze to everyone's amusement. I put the glass down quickly, mortified.

The dark teak wood table gleamed and shone, I could see my face on it. The cook was in a frenzy running between the kitchen and the dining table with piping hot bowls and plates of food. Cooked and served instantly. Each dish a visual master piece of colour, delicate and delectable. The variety endless.

Apart from the usual pork, chicken and fish, there were sea cucumbers, sea weed, shark fin and a variety of delicacies I had never seen or heard of. They had all been brought by Mr. King, all the way from Hong Kong. What fascinated me most, were the 100 years old eggs. Hen's eggs treated and buried under the earth, they had turned a dark brown, the white of the egg translucent.

It was most frustrating to look and wonder how I was going to eat it all with just two long sticks. Ma and I were put out of our misery by Mrs. King who provided us with forks.

The Chinese did not serve themselves from the dishes but merrily carried on helping themselves directly with their chopsticks from which ever dish took their fancy. They did not seem to have any qualms about putting the chop sticks into their mouths and then back again into the bowl of food making it *jutha*. So this is what Bahadur had warned me about, I was too hungry to contemplate on such matters so I too, dug my used fork into whatever I pleased!

Mrs. King had got used to her life in Monjula by now but when she heard we would be spending the three months of my winter holidays in Calcutta, she promptly decided to accompany us.

Ma spent days packing our umpteen trunks and bedding for our long sojourn. Mrs. King believed in traveling light. The old American Chevrolet was hired to take us to Siliguri to catch the Darjeeling Mail. I hated this car. The thick padded, soiled upholstery reeked of petrol and dozens of awful smells. I would get sick and feel miserable by the time I got down to Teesta.

The road to Siliguri was always damp. It never saw the light of day being completely covered by the thick canopy of trees. The deep, dark, forest continued endlessly. The peculiar dank smell of rotting vegetation added to my misery. Oh, how I hated this three hour long drive. I would arrive at Siliguri limp with exhaustion.

We were cruising along at good speed when the huge, heavy car spluttered and stopped in the middle of nowhere. There were no shops or villages along the way. We just drove on and on through the dark tunnel of trees.

The experienced driver tinkered with the car for what seemed hours but couldn't get it to come back to life. We were stranded.

It was getting darker by the minute. The mighty forest's orchestra had started. The shrill long whine of crickets and the beat produced by hooting of owls. Myriads of sounds, soft, low or high pitched from various insects filled the forest air. The fireflies not to be out done lit up the darkness with their tiny glows of florescent lights. It was an exclusive performance of sound and light never to be repeated or experienced again in my life.

While I was enjoying the sights and sounds of the night, ma was getting nervous and agitated. We would surely miss the train, spending the night cramped up in this car, in the middle of the forest. We could become the meal of nocturnal animals.

Hardly any cars plied on this road certainly not after dark. We saw a beam of light and then a car. Our driver stopped the car and asked for help. Hill drivers always go out of their way to help each other but this one sped away to our great disappointment.

Ma asked the driver why the other driver didn't want to help us. The single occupant of the car was in a mighty hurry to catch the Darjeeling Mail so he couldn't be bothered giving us a lift the driver explained. "Who was the gentleman?" ma asked. The manager *sahib,* of the Das Bank in Kalimpong. Ma was furious. She knew this manager very well. "This is no way for a gentleman to behave," she screamed. Our fate was sealed.

At last we heard a rumbling in the distance. Soon, a huge army truck rumbled up and stopped by us. A bunch of young British soldiers jumped out and peered at us through the windows of our car. Ma begged them to give us a lift till Siliguri.

They were more than happy, in fact, delighted to do so. In a thrice they lifted our heavy trunks, as if they were cardboard cartons and flung them in the back of their truck. Then hoisted ma and me into the back as well but invited Mrs. King to join the driver and his mates up front. They turned a deaf ear to Mrs. King's protests to join them. They were hefty, young, gum chewing, crew cut, lobster red soldiers.

They couldn't have set eyes on a female for months specially not one as young and pretty as Mrs. King. They were determined to seat her in front. When coaxing and cajoling didn't work, they lifted her bodily. This is when she screamed "*Didi*! *Didi*!" for ma's help.

Ma, never agile or athletic, in desperation, managed to jump down from the high back seat and ran to save her. There ensued a tug-of war. Ma was losing the battle against these hefty young men so she let out a volley of well aimed barbed verbal shot. "How dare you manhandle this young lady? Don't you have any shame? You young soldiers are here to protect us not to harm us. How can you pick on helpless women, go find someone your size. Is this what you have learnt in the British army? Is this what your parents taught you? Is this valour and honour your Generals are so proud of?" they let go of Mrs. King, jumped into the truck, heads down, cursing under their breath.

The rest of the way we sat huddled in the back. Mrs. King was shaking with frights as ma held her tight. "You are safe now," she kept repeating. We could hear the driver swearing loudly as he drove furiously all the way to Siliguri.

Luckily the train hadn't left when we were unceremoniously dumped at the station. We occupied our berths in the first class compartment and settled down, much relieved that the nightmare was over at last.

Suddenly the door opened and in breezed the Das Bank Manager full of smiles. "Oh, *Didi* you are here, how nice to see you." "Nice to see me indeed. You passed us in your empty car but didn't give us a lift. You call yourself a gentleman, leaving helpless ladies in the jungle?" "Oh, I am so sorry I didn't know it was you in the car." "Of course you knew; now go away, I don't want to see your face."

I was surprised at these strong words coming out of ma's mouth for the second time this evening. "*Didi*, please, please forgive me. I have been called to Calcutta suddenly, all the berths are booked. Can you please let me have your child's berth?" "How can you have the audacity to ask me for such a favour? I suppose you thought you would get all our berths if we didn't make it."

He whined and pleaded until ma's kindness won over her anger and he got my berth. I had to sleep on a make shift bed of piled up trunks next to ma's berth.

Growing Up Pains

Dr. Robi Som and his wife, Kana, lived in one of the flats at Kanchanjungha *Kothi*. Dr. Som worked in the Kalimpong Agriculture Farm. An energetic young man, he was always in demand to organize various social functions. Kanadi, a good house wife and mother, held fort while her husband went on tours. The young couple with two small children were constant visitors at Monjula and soon became a part of our family.

The two children, a boy of five Bacchu and a two year old girl Nanu, didn't interest me at all, being much younger than myself. They were very sweet, affectionate and well behaved little children. They played quietly in the garden and didn't disturb the elders. They were model children alright.

When Lady Abala Bose, my aunt, wife of Sir J.C. Bose, passed away in Calcutta, baba sent for ma. Since I couldn't miss school, I had to be left behind in Kalimpong. Kanadi, always helpful, volunteered to come and stay at Monjula to look after me. Ma was relieved. Kanadi arrived with her two children. An efficient housewife, she took charge of Monjula, me and life went on smoothly.

Bacchu a quiet, gentle, sober little boy started being obstinate and rebellious for some unknown reason. He had not started school so his mother took great pains to tutor him at home. He was a bright boy, learnt fast and enjoyed his daily lessons but suddenly refused to study. He played and ran around the garden all day long to his mother's consternation.

All coaxing, cajoling and threats were of no avail. He continued to be un-cooperative and difficult.

When I got back from school he would follow me around. I ignored him. One evening he went berserk. He climbed the low roof of the outhouse where bottles of *achars* were left out for sunning and in a fit of temper, smashed them all. Both Kanadi and I heard the noise and rushed out of the house to investigate.

The *masala,* soaked red chilies, strips of mangoes, *jalpais,* lay scattered on the tin roof, covered by a shower of glistening splintered glass. The rich, golden yellow, viscous mustard oil made its way down the corrugated tin roof and dripped lazily on the ground below. The mouth watering aroma of *achars* filled the air.

Bacchu was caught red-handed. He was trying to scramble down from the roof without much success, slipping and sliding on the mustard oil.

Kanadi's usually serene, fair face turned red with rage as she took in the scene at a glance. She ran out of the house, grabbed Bacchu but now being fully immersed in the delicious mustard oil, he slipped out of her grasp and ran down the steps that led to the lower lawn. She in her voluminous *saree,* was no match for the spirited little boy running for his life.

When she couldn't catch up with him, she stood with hands on her hips, huffing and puffing, threatening him with dire consequences. With a safe distance between him and his mother he stood still and cheekily stuck out his tongue at her.

This insolence added insult to injury. Kanadi, seething with anger, hitched up her flapping *saree,* higher, gathered all her energy and with her last wind made a hundred meter dash towards him. He neatly evaded the charge with the expertise of an experienced matador and ran back, up the stairs as fast as his little legs could carry him, stopping only to pick up pebbles, on the way, to fling on the window panes of the outhouse. The shattered glass panes tinkled down merrily to rest on the window ledge.

This was his last act of defiance; he had run out of steam and ideas. His punishment lasted for two whole days until he sobered down completely and regretted his misadventure.

Kanadi was mortified and worried as to how she was going to break the news of the smashed *achar* bottles to ma.

I suppose, I was wholly to blame for ignoring this little boy who was craving for my attention and friendship. The only way he thought he could get it was to do something spectacular. Well I was impressed. We became the best friends from then till now.

Bacchu's real name is Himachal Som. An Indian ambassador. He is also the father of Vishnu Som, the news reader of NDTV.

Kanadi, an industrious housewife, kept herself busy all day. No relaxation or afternoon nap for her. She would spend the afternoon knitting or embroidering pillow cases and table cloths. She would sit on the verandah with ma's work basket full of needles, skeins of thread, buttons, scissors and other odds and ends which had no business to be there. Ma was not the tidiest of persons so all kinds of unrelated things found their way into her spacious work basket and lived there happily ever after.

In the evening Bacchu and Nanu were running around on the lawn when suddenly Nanu bent double clutching her stomach. Her face wracked with pain, I sprinted across the lawn just in time to pick her up, gather her in my arms and deposit her on her mother's lap.

Kanadi rubbed her little stomach, until she relaxed a little. Although she couldn't talk but could make signs and utter a few words, she now pointed to the toilet door. After the first evacuation she felt much relieved but soon the trips to the toilet became fast and furious. She was drained out. Kanadi tried to rock her to sleep on her lap. Nanu's bright little face was waning. Her eyelids were almost transparent. She moaned through dry lips.

There were no medicines in the house to stop the raging diarrhea. It was getting dark. The only young male, our cook, had left for home. Nanu's father Somda was out of town on tour. Our ayah and Kanadi were the only adults in the house. There were no phones or cars to send a message to Dr. Boral to come. He lived miles away in town.

Our few neighbours were old retired people who must have been getting ready for bed while we sat helplessly in the middle of a crisis. Nanu lay on her mother's lap limp as a rag doll, scarcely breathing. Kanadi had been brave and strong so far but as Nanu's condition gradually deteriorated, she was panicking.

Bacchu and I sat and watched silently. Bacchu's large black eyes reaching the proportion of saucers, whispered to me, "Is she going to die?" he had no concept of death neither did I? "Of course not," I whispered back in a wavering voice, trying desperately to hold back tears that were threatening to spill over.

Nanu's feet were turning cold. The ayah started massaging them vigorously. Kanadi was spooning drops of water through

Nanu's parched lips. Kanadi's face was white as a sheet, hair disheveled and tears poured down her cheeks as she loudly evoked every god she could think of to save her poor little baby. Bacchu bewildered and upset to see his mother's state, started to howl. Mother and son's wailing in different keys sounded like a funeral dirge.

Suddenly Nanu's eyelids flickered and opened slightly. Colour was coming back to her pale cheeks. She moaned and kicked her legs. The worst was over and so were our fears. It was not cholera. The cups of water that Kanadi had pumped into her must have done the trick. We heaved a sigh of relief.

Once Nanu slept peacefully, Kanadi and I were debating as to what had caused the diarrhea. We had all eaten the same food. Then it struck me. I ran to fetch ma's needle work basket. I opened it and fished out a small flat box of Booklax. It was empty. The tin had contained a whole miniature slab of purgative which looked, smelt and tasted like chocolate to fool children into taking them.

The mystery was solved. While Kanadi was busy with her embroidery that afternoon, Nanu had been fiddling with the contents of the work basket. She had alighted upon the delicious little chocolates and made a meal of them. She had been fooled alright!

Nanu turned out to be a wonderful human being, much loved. She passed away a few years back but the Brooklax episode still lives on.

The Roerichs of Kalimpong

I remember ma, dragging me, at a tender age, to tea parties given by Mrs. Helena Roerich at Crookety. I hated these tea parties as there were no children to play with. I had to sit quietly for hours like a wooden doll, as well behaved children were supposed to do, while ma and Mrs. Roerich talked endlessly on matters which went right over my head and bored me to tears. They had much in common. They were both interested in the upliftment of women.

These long spells of inactivity, in a straight jacket, gave me ample chance to study the inhabitants of the house. The only part of the body that I could move, without disapproval of the elders, were my eyes. There were three people in the house and they were quaint as the house itself.

Betty Sheriff built her dream house and called it Crookety. It was right out of a fairy tale. I loved it. It was the most beautiful house that I had ever seen. The red tiles on the steep, soaring roof were tightly knitted like fish scales. The beauty of the house lay in its sharp inverted V shaped roofs creating a range of peaks on top. The roof came plunging down steeply, encasing the top floor bedrooms giving them slanting walls. The two roofs over the porch one slimmer than the other, were so low, that they touched my head. Black, steel framed windows opened out into the manicured walled garden with a lily pool full of gold fish.

The spacious drawing room with its oval fireplace always welcomed us with a blazing fire. The bright and airy study faced the front garden and the Kanchanjunga. The dining room was in line with these two rooms down the passage, spacious and bright opening on to a verandah which also served the study as well. A short flight of steps led up to the bedrooms upstairs. The service staircase in the dining room led to the bedrooms for the servants to go up unobtrusively, to take-up bed tea, breakfast trays and for cleaning up. A house designed to perfection for maximum comfort and a decadent life style.

I was always wary of the highly polished slippery wooden floors. The drawing room was warm and cozy with comfortable silk upholstered chairs, priceless woollen carpets, crystals and the delicate Chinese vases. Mrs. Helena Roerich reigned supreme in this room. She just filled the room with her presence.

She was a small lady but with a regal bearing keeping with her aristocrat background. Her great, great grandfather was Mikhail Kutuzo the Field Marshal who led the Russian army against Napoleon. Her aunt was princess Putyatine with whom she spent many a summer picking up court etiquette.

Mrs. Helena Roerich lived in Crookety with her elder son Yuri, George and an adopted daughter. Mrs. Roerich and her son looked old as the hills to me but the daughter was a lissome young lady. They were fair skinned people and I had seen many such but there was something different about them. They had higher cheek bones I thought.

George Roerich was stockily built. He always wore a grey woollen suit which matched his pepper and salt hair and beard. From my perch I would admire his highly polished, mirror finished, black shoes while his mother's were just as shiny but pointed, slim lady's shoes. Her long dress reached her shoes, worn over layers of petticoats which added to her girth. The long sleeves reached her wrists.

Always draped in a black mantilla which loosely hung from her frail shoulders, she floated around the spacious drawing room in a flurry with a swish of her voluminous clothing. Not a single strand of her brown hair was out of place but sternly swept back, to end in a small tight *khopa,* at the back of her head clasped by a wide gold clip.

Her daughter, a young lady, wore her dark hair parted in the middle and wound around the back of her head neatly. She wore loose gathered skirts which reached well below the knees. She was very sweet and gentle, rather shy as she could not speak much English. She was aware of my discomfort amongst adults and would take me for a walk in the gorgeous garden full of exotic plants and flowers, to look at the gold fish flitting amongst the lilies in the pond.

Ma in her turn was equally considerate towards her and invited her to all our picnics and outings as the Roerich mother and son never went out on such frivolous and energetic outings. She did enjoy these outings very much as being confined in a house with two elderly intellectual people could be trying at times.

As for me, the best part of the tea party was when tea was served. The tea came in a Russian silver urn sitting on a silver tray along with delicate bone china cups and saucers. Another tray arrived laden with mouth watering, light as a feather, pastries, cakes, biscuits and a host of other goodies, all baked expertly, at home, according to Mrs. Helena Roerich's Russian recipes. Ma kept a strict watch on me to see that I did not make a pig of myself or drop the delicate china in my eagerness to pile up my plate.

George the grey man, in a grey suit, would appear for tea then make polite conversation, excuse himself and disappear in to the book lined study, next door, to busy himself with his writing and painting. He was a great Tibetan scholar and had come to live in Kalimpong because his Tibetan Guru lived here.

Helena came to Kalimpong to stay with her son George, his younger brother, Svyatoslav also came to Kalimpong to visit them with his beautiful, famous, Indian film star wife, Devika Rani. She was the grand niece of Rabindranath Tagore. Whenever she came to Kalimpong, the local people would hang around the roads to get a glimpse of her taking a walk with her husband.

I do remember getting a glimpse of the beautiful star taking a walk with her Russian husband. I was so engrossed by her that I completely missed her husband walking beside her. He must have been a real charmer, to have wooed and won the hand of the leading lady of the silver screen. I would love to know more about this great romance. I wonder if there is a record of it. He was a renowned painter.

Helena came to visit her son George, three times in Kalimpong and her last visit ended here. She died on 5th October 1955 and I remember ma going to her funeral at Durpin where she was buried. What better place than the highest point of the mountain, to be in eternal peace facing the Kanchanjunga.

Many years later I visited Nagar in Kulu and was surprised to find the Roerich museum there. The wooden cottage once belonged to Nicholas Roerich, Helena's husband. They arrived from Russia in 1928 with their two sons and lived there in Nagar.

Nicholas Roerich was a versatile genius of Russia, interested in the Indian Vedic culture. He was a marvelous painter and the museum is full of his paintings of the Himalayas, in all its moods, captured by him on canvas. He was a great scholar so was his wife. Together they authored many books. Helena wrote on ethical and spiritual subjects especially on the importance of the woman's role in the new era. She is best known for her book Agni Yoga.

She now has scores of Italians and people from other countries too who religiously follow her Art of Living. Crookety has become a meditation centre. People who follow her teachings abroad come here in big groups to meditate.

They invariably manage to locate me as I happen to be one of the very few lucky people left who had the privilege of meeting this great lady, their guru. They are only too eager to listen to whatever little I remember about her. They even invited me to visit their headquarters in Italy which I did.

Nicholas Roerich's greatest contribution to the world was the Roerich pact, signed at the White hall in 1935 by twenty countries. Now 60 countries are signatories of this pact. This pact prohibits warring nations from attacking churches, museums, hospitals and historical buildings during war wherever Roerich's banner of peace is flown. The banner is white with three red spheres enclosed in a circle. The three spheres symbolized the past present and future. What a marvelous idea to preserve heritage buildings of each country during mindless destruction.

That pact was signed before the Second World War; perhaps it was instrumental in saving the most important pieces of architecture in Europe and England during the war. I wonder, if those precious old buildings of Kalimpong would have been spared if they flew the Roerich flag atop of them to preserve the heritage of Kalimpong for posterity. But then, what does a simple flag signify to ignorant marauding rabble? Does Roerich's flag, so brilliantly conceived have any place in this day and age of terrorist maniacs and nuclear warfare??

We Indians are so proud to have had such a brilliant Russian family of scholars living in India and contributing so much towards art and literature for the whole world.

To keep the memories of the Roerichs alive, the Consul General of the Federation of Russia has promised us a Roerich Museum in Kalimpong soon, in the lines of the one in Nagar in Kulu.

Loshay Untamed

Reverend George Patterson, the handsome young Scottish Missionary, arrived in Kalimpong with just the clothes on his back and a *Khampa,* slave in tow. He had fled from Lhasa, Tibet, in a hurry, to avoid the Chinese invasion. The only route open to him was the mule trail to Kalimpong, over the Himalayas and Jelapla Pass into India.

Loshay the strapping, wild, young *Khampa,* had refused to leave his master. He had followed and protected him, saving his life many times through the difficult, treacherous route infested with fiery brigands.

Patterson was relieved to be in a safe haven at last so he decided to stay on and rented a flat, next door to us, at Chitrabhanu. He claimed to be a preacher. He did not have the excuse of leaning Tibetan to live in Kalimpong like all the other foreigners, of that time, since he spoke Tibetan fluently. He therefore, decided to write books about his adventures in Tibet in the solitude of Kalimpong. He did write a number of books but I remember only two, "God's Fool" and "Tibetan Journey" which he had presented to ma.

Patterson slim, slight with long brown wavy hair and beard, twinkling blue eyes was quite charming with a great sense of humour and a broad Scottish accent which I found difficult to understand.

With all these qualities he soon became the life and soul of the foreigners gathering in the Himalayan Hotel every evening with Annie Perry as their amiable hostess.

As his social life progressed, his domestic life deteriorated. His faithful slave Loshay, extremely loyal and faithful, belonging to the warrior tribe couldn't be tamed or domesticated. He was the product of the wild; fierce and brutal in war. He guarded his master with his life and soul but couldn't sustain his master's life by producing a simple omelet.

The untamed, uncouth, uncivilized boor became the bane of Pattersons's life, he failed to tame him. He would never become the gentleman's gentleman.

Almost every morning, Loshay would come bounding up our garden path in his *bokhu,* knee high Tibetan boots, a long dagger, swinging from his belt and a charming smile, displaying strong, white, even teeth. The purpose of these visits were to borrow sugar, tea, flour, eggs, just about anything that he had forgotten to buy.

He refused to discard his *bokhu* and boots in spite of the hot weather and he would rather give up his life than his dagger.

His cooking skills were nonexistent so Patterson grew thinner by the day. Ma realizing his plight would send him whatever was cooked to supplement his inedible lunch.

I would often sneak into Loshay's kitchen to watch him in action. He hated being confined to the kitchen. He preferred to be outdoors. A son of the vast open country, trained to be a warrior not a cook or house maid.

Loshay blundered around in the kitchen like a bull in a china shop. He flung pots and pans around making a terrible racket. He was born with knuckle dusters on his hands. Cups, saucers, plates just disintegrated in his big hands. Cutlery was all twisted out of shape, broken or completely disappeared. He would pick up the broken pieces and aim them into the dustbin with great accuracy.

The rubbish dump in the garden soon filled up with broken cutlery, crockery, dented burnt pots and pans disfigured beyond recognition, diligently buried by the *mali*, to be discovered by posterity. Any archeologist who discovers this treasure trove will spend months figuring out what these objects were originally.

He looked down on all kitchen knives disdainfully. He used his long dagger to hack up unwashed, unpeeled vegetables or to dismember a whole chicken. The pieces flew around in all directions. The head out of the open window, the leg in the sink full of dirty dishes. He would pick up the pieces and dump then in a pan to boil. He was too impatient to let them boil till cooked so if he left the kitchen, they would burn to cinders along with the pot!

Once, he was viciously jabbing at a can of sausages with a table knife to open it, the knife didn't make the slightest dent but the steel blade parted company from the bone handle. He looked at the handle with disgust and slammed it into the bin. He unsheathed his dagger, laid the can horizontally on the table and with one mighty blow, split the can in two. He turned and smiled at me proudly. I clapped my hands and nodded in approval.

Patterson was always invited to every party. He felt that he had to reciprocate so he decided to throw a tea party. He invited Prince Peter, Nebesky his secretary, Princess Kesang Dorji, now the queen mother of Bhutan, a number of foreigners, ma and me.

Inviting people was easy. Food was not a problem. Our cook was going to produce most of the dishes required.

Delicious sponge cakes from Gompus and a variety of sweets from the town. The only problem was the cutlery and crockery required for the party. Patterson possibly couldn't serve his august guests food on chipped plates and give them an assortment of twisted cutlery to eat with. His only recourse was to approach ma.

Ma always eager to help people in distress was aghast when Patterson asked her to lend him her best tea set complete with silver cutlery just for one evening.

Ma was well aware of Loshay's congenital knuckle duster hands and his ingenuity of demolishing even the toughest of pots and pans. She could visualize her precious eggshell china, brought from Japan many years ago, crumbling in his hands like wafer and her polished silver cutlery carefully preserved, misshaped and scarred! This picture in ma's mind was too real so her reply was a flat "No."

Patterson was not to be so easily dismissed. He begged and pleaded with ma promising, to warn Loshay to be very, very careful. Ma parted with her best Japanese tea set reluctantly with a heavy heart.

We arrived at the tea party to find everything well laid out. Loshay was doing a good job of serving good food. Ma's heart was in her mouth when Loshay arrived with a tray piled with her precious set. He poured the tea into the cups and served each guest swaggering amongst the small tea tables in his cumbersome *bokhu,* his long swinging dagger threatening to sweep off everything from the tables.

Needless to say, ma was on tenter-hooks and didn't enjoy the party. She was expecting to see her precious crockery come crashing down. Fortunately no such disaster occurred. The party was a great success.

Next morning Loshay arrived at Monjula with his usual broad charming smile to return the borrowed goods. Two egg-shell china cups and three saucers were missing. The milk jug had lost its handle. The spout of the tea pot displayed a jaggered end. Ma collapsed in agony!

Patterson was thoroughly ashamed when told of his dear Loshay's handiwork and offered to replace the broken items. That was just not possible because Japan had long stopped manufacturing this particular type of china with its beautiful blue motif. It was a rare set. I still have some of it.

Loshay was quick tempered, since he couldn't understand the local lingo, he took it for granted that everyone was insulting him. He settled all arguments by his dagger. People were terrified of this smiling, hefty man who in the blink of an eye turned from a good-natured genial guy to a blood thirsty murderous lunatic. Hot blood coursed through his veins so did his lust for the fairer sex. He was very sweet to the maids and other women he met.

One evening on his way back home from the market, he had grabbed a woman walking on the road. Her terrified screams had brought all the men in that area to her rescue. They had beaten Loshay senseless and then dragged him to the police station and got him locked up. They couldn't have got him there in any other state.

Patterson was not overly worried when Loshay didn't turn up that night. Very often he disappeared at night, like a tom cat and appeared grinning next morning without displaying any ill effects from his nocturnal adventure.

Next morning a constable arrived to inform Patterson that Loshay was languishing in the lock up and he would have to go and bail him out.

Loshay was always getting into trouble but this time he had gone too far. Patterson was furious and came to consult ma. She had no sympathy for Loshay. She advised Patterson not to let him out but let him sweat it out in jail for a few days to mend his wayward, impulsive, irresponsible ways.

"Patterson, he is always giving you trouble. Why don't you put your foot down for once?" ma asked.

"*Didi,* he is just an over grown fun loving exuberant child, he means no harm. He is loyal, faithful and has saved my life several times at the risk of losing his. He regards me as his father, mother, lord and master. How can I be hard on him?"

"Well indulge him some more, you will be sorry the day he kills somebody"!

Patterson found a belligerent Loshay in the small lock up, bellowing like an enraged bull, flailing his arms like a windmill, breathing fire and brimstone. Determined to kill all those rascals who had shoved him into this hell hole, including all those stupid khaki clad men.

Patterson determined to know what happened and why he had got locked up asked him for an explanation. "I did nothing wrong master. I don't know why these people beat me and locked me up" stated Loshay innocently.

"You must have done something terrible now tell me what?" asked Patterson determined to get at the truth.

"Well, I was walking back home from the market, late in the evening when I noticed a young woman in front of me. She was well dressed, looked beautiful as she walked swaying her hips from side to side. Master, I have never ever seen such a beautiful woman in the whole of Kalimpong before. I came to the conclusion that she was not real at all but a beautiful *churel,* out to entice men like me. I swear to you, master, I meant no harm. All I wanted to do was to grab that *churel,* to prove whether she was a ghost or not. I walked stealthily behind her, she was not aware how close I was to her and then with a leap and a bound I caught her and clasped her in my arms. Unfortunately she was a real woman of flesh and blood. See how she has scratched me with her nails all over my face and arms? Then she screamed like a banshee, waking up the whole village. They came in hordes. You know master, how easily I can dispose off several men at a time but they came well armed with *khukuris,* sticks and stones. They hit me on the head, then I knew no more. Now tell me, master, what did I do to receive such treatment by these stupid little gutless men?"

This was a likely story that Patterson didn't believe but there was not much he could do except warn Loshay to stay away from all woman *churel,* or not. He had had to pay heavily for this misadventure of Loshay's.

Patterson went away on a long holiday and came back with a beautiful young wife to Loshay's surprise and ours. He found his Scottish bride in Ludhiana and not Scotland! She was a highly qualified surgeon. The young couple was not destined to live happily ever after but Loshay was the only spoke in their wheel.

All Mrs. Patterson's attempt to run the house smoothly and properly were foiled, intentionally or unintentionally, by Loshay's blunders. He was loyal to his lord and master but who was this slip of a white woman to order him around. So he did what he pleased causing misunderstanding between husband and wife. Most disturbing of all was that his beloved master was besotted by this woman. He felt neglected, ignored and insecure.

Mrs Patterson, a gentle soul, found it impossible to handle Loshay but her husband refused to take any action against him, no matter what misdeed or mischief he indulged in.

The couple went back to Scotland to settle down. Ma was shocked to learn that Loshay was going to accompany them. She predicted disaster. She begged Patterson not to take Loshay with him. He would be a total misfit there. The authorities there would not take kindly to his antics and outrageous behaviour. He would be a source of headache and embarrassment to him.

Patterson adamant as usual, where Loshay was concerned, took him to Scotland. He brought him back to Kalimpong within three months and left him behind for good.

Ma was right, he was back in Kalimpong very soon but we did not see him. We heard that he had got a job in Dr. Graham's Homes bakery.

Many years later while visiting the bakery, I suddenly remembered that Loshay worked there so I asked to see him. After a long wait, a short, thin, shabbily dressed man in a grubby apron appeared.

"I would like to meet Loshay," I said to him. "I am Loshay," he replied. "Patterson's Loshay?" I asked incredulously. "Yes" I couldn't believe my eyes.

The huge, strong, carefree, dashing daredevil with ruddy cheeks and bulging muscles minus his *bokhu,* high boots and long dagger just couldn't be Loshay. Standing demurely with drooping shoulder, graying hair and sunken cheeks. He seemed to have shrunk or had I grown? Just then he recognized me, and his face lit up for a second with that angelic smile I remembered so well, although it had lost its spontaneity.

He told me that he was married to a local girl and had produced several children. He was the master baker in the Homes. He produced excellent bread.

His eyes misted over as he talked about Patterson, his beloved master. He often dreamt of those carefree days when they rode together in the Himalayas as father qand son not as master and slave. Patterson had never treated him as a slave but as a son.

A sense of sadness brought tears to my eyes as I remembered the strapping young specimen of a man, bursting with energy and vitality, now reduced to a frail, sober, lifeless nonentity.

Patterson had failed to tame this wild creature but it was bread that did it!

Courteous Burglar

The monsoon rains thundered down each night on our tin roof sounding like a hundred galloping horses. Darkness enveloped everything outside, only to be lit up occasionally by bursts of incandescent lightning, followed by deafening thunder claps. I hated these terrifying nights and clung closer to ma.

The dacoits took advantage of such a night to invade the house of Mr. Pradhan at 11th Mile. *Chors* and dacoits were non-existent in Kalimpong then. Mr. Pradhan and his family were rudely woken one night by the sound of their front door being battered down. The three men of the house rushed downstairs with whatever objects they had at hand, to beat up the drunk they expected to find. Mr. Pradhan had grabbed a walking stick, his brother an umbrella and his son a boot.

The dacoits had already entered the house. Masked men in black berets. Only their eyes were visible. The Pradhans were taken aback. "What do you want?" asked Mr. Pradhan. "Everything," was the answer. At this the three men brandishing their weapons fell on the men bravely, making a stand, to ward off these unwelcome visitors in the middle of the night.

Although totally outnumbered, it did not deter them from taking a few whacks at the intruders. The dacoits wrenched away their puny weapons with infinite ease. A fistfight followed, interrupted by much shouting and swearing until the leader of the gang pulled out a gun and pointed it at

Mr. Pradhan. Dead silence followed. They went about tying up the three Pradhans and two servants securely to chairs and started methodically ransacking all the rooms downstairs.

Upstairs, the ladies were quick to pluck the children from their cozy beds, bundling them and dumping them under the big bed in the master bedroom. Last of all hobbled in old Granny. They shut and barricaded the door after her.

Granny figured that the dacoits hadn't come to terrorize or molest the women and children. They had come to steal. She opened the two large wooden *almirahs,* in the room, scooped out the gold and silver ornaments and flung them out the window as far as her frail arms would allow. She ordered every woman to take off her gold chains, bangles etc. And do likewise. She took out bundles of currency notes and stuffed them under a small *morah.* She was smart enough to leave a few bundles behind. She went and sat calmly on the *morah,* the ladies sat on the bed nervously, while the children peered from under the bed terrified.

The dacoits having finished their business downstairs made their way up leisurely. This delay had given Granny ample time to do the disappearing act with the jewellery and cash.

They burst into the master bedroom after delivering a mighty kick on the flimsy door. Their eyes went straight to the wooden *almirahs.* The leader spoke in Hindi, not Nepali. "Please give me the keys of the *almirahs,*" he requested softly, to no one in particular. The ladies were taken aback. This short little man, dressed like a menacing pirate, spoke like a kind gentleman. The stark terror that had paralyzed them now loosened its grip. They breathed easier.

Mrs. Pradhan took the bunch of keys from under the pillow and handed them to him. The first *almirah,* yielded nothing but clothes, shoes, papers, files, other odds and ends but no money or jewellery. He attacked the second one with vigour. They were in no hurry. The men of the house were securely tied up. They couldn't possibly raise an alarm. The nearest house was a mile away. There was no unnecessary gadget like telephones. Each house was an island in the middle of orange orchards and rice fields.

Since the dacoits did not expect any interruption, they carried on their operation with great deliberation. They had all the time in the world. To their disgust, the second *almirah,* only yielded a few bundles of Rs. 10 notes, a few silver coins, children's earning, rings, watches and a thin gold chain overlooked by Granny.

This was a small fortune then but they had expected to find a huge amount of gold and cash. In fact they had perfect knowledge of the Pradhan's wealth. That is why they had struck there. Convinced that the Pradhan's wealth was hidden not in the *almirah*s but somewhere else, the leader barked staccato orders in Hindi to his men to fan out and search every inch of the house thoroughly.

The men stripped the beds, slit the mattress, quilts and pillows, opened all trunks, suitcases and dragged the petrified children from under the bed. During all this commotion, Granny sat in the corner on her *morah,* silently counting her beads with great concentration. The men didn't even bother to glance at the old lady lost in prayer.

The incessant rain had abated. Dawn would make its appearance soon. The leader decided to call it a day. Their well planned strike was a failure. They couldn't fathom why. They had done their homework well. They had watched the Pradhan's house carefully, knew all their movements and knew that they kept their money and jewellery at home.

There were no lockers in the solitary Das Bank. *Chors* and dacoits were unheard of so people kept their valuables at home. The Pradhans were just the people for easy picking, as were many others. Disappointed and angry they left reluctantly.

At dawn the milkman was surprised to find the orange tree next to the Pradhan's house, decorated like a Christmas tree! Gold chains, necklaces and bangles hung from the branches, twinkling in the rays of the rising sun! Granny's presence of mind had saved the day.

The dacoits struck again and again. The people of Kalimpong lived in terror. The meager police force was totally out of depth to apprehend this bold gun toting brigand. All that they had gathered from plundered houses were that these men were from the plains.

They were six or more in number. Their chief was a gentleman who went about his business politely. He had absolute control over his men and made sure they did not resort to any violence or indecency. They only raided the far flung houses of the rich. All this information amounted to nothing; the police were clueless.

While the whole of Kalimpong lived in fear, ma was unconcerned. She maintained that even though she lived in a big house like Monjula with just a maid, a cook and me, she was not rich, the dacoits would not waste their time raiding her house. They were very clever they had only targeted the rich people.

Her perception of their thinking process sounded logical to me. I slowly lost the goose flesh and nightmares of hooded men I was having every night. The attacks stopped just as suddenly as they had started. Months went by without any incident and the people of Kalimpong heaved a sigh of relief.

One morning a scruffy and unkempt young man in deep thought was seen walking up and down in Thana Dara, just below the Kalimpong police station. He suddenly bounded up the short flight of stairs of the police station and wished to see the OC.

The OC's apathy turned to interest and excitement as he listened to the young man's tale. He claimed to be a member of the gang of dacoits who had held Kalimpong in their grip. He was not afraid of punishment, all he wanted was justice. Revenge was his ultimate aim. The reason was simple. The gang had cheated him. They had not given him an equal portion of the booty as promised.

He was a godsend. The OC had visions of name, fame, promotion and may be a medal or two. His picture in the newspapers. He would surely make headlines and his brave exploits printed in detail for apprehending the most wanted, dreaded gang of dacoits terrorizing Kalimpong.

The OC was shocked to learn that the leader of the gang had fallen in love with Kalimpong and settled down with his family in Bong Basti under his very nose. More shocking was the fact that he was none other than the short, soft spoken, gentle, middle-aged, retired schoolteacher, Sudhirbabu, whom he knew well! It took a lot of convincing by the young man before the OC reluctantly decided to search Sudhirbabu's house and question him. He threatened the young man with dire consequence if Sudhirbabu was found innocent.

The OC arrived at Sudhirbabu's little hut with a small posse of policemen. Sudhirbabu greeted him genially and gladly invited him to search his humble dwelling. The policemen set to work while the OC and Sudhirbabu sat outside sipping tea. The OC found out that Sudhirbabu was a Communist! He had taken early retirement as he was fed up of the capitalist world. He wanted to live a simple life and so he settled in Kalimpong. He gave tuitions to make ends meet.

The hut was small with very few belongings so the search was over soon. They found nothing to incriminate Sudhirbabu.

Dejected with the futile search and aware of the jibes they would have to face for their wild goose chase; one policeman was trying to calm his nerves by smoking a *bidi*, at the kitchen door. He vented his anger on a pile of firewood by the earthen *chulas,* giving it a mighty kick with his heavy boot. The heavy logs crashed down on the *chulas*, demolishing them.

Sudhirbabu's wife screamed at the policeman for destroying her *chulas*. Sheepishly he apologized profusely and was beating a hasty retreat when the corner of his eye caught a glint in the debris. He turned on his heels, shoved his hand in the debris and pulled it out. It was a solid, shining gold chain!

The *chulas* and the mud floor of the kitchen were soon dug up to reveal gold, gold and more gold! Stacks of currency notes were found in small tin boxes. A king's ransom. They also found a toy gun and note book containing full details of the whole operation.

The men had arrived from the plains and rented an obscure little house just below Monjula. From here they had surveyed Kalimpong and Sudhirbabu, the gentle dacoit, had masterminded the whole operation brilliantly and carried it out to perfection.

The first page of the note book carried a hit list of the houses in Kalimpong. Monjula topped the list. It was the only house spared. Intrigued the OC asked Sudhirbabu why it was left out. He smiled and said, "I am a great admirer of Jyoti Basu so how could I rob his cousin, Mrs. Mitter house?" When jail sentence was imminent Sudhirbabu went stark mad. This was the last bit of his superb acting!

Jyoti Basu heard this story and very proudly related it to all and sundry how Monjula was saved from being robbed because of him. Ma was grateful to him and luckily she died long before her beloved Monjula was burnt down due to her unfortunately being related to Jyoti Basu.

The Mule Train

The most positive outcome of Mr. Vajpayee's recent visit to China was the joint agreement between the two countries, to open the trade routes between India and China once again. This trade route existed between Tibet and India since time immemorial but records put it down around 1883–84. Unfortunately, this route was discontinued from 1960 just before the Chinese aggression in 1962. Since them the armies of India and China stand eye ball to eye ball on Nathula Pass. Trade, a long forgotten thing of the past.

Two trade routes existed both from Chumbi Valley in Tibet. One via Nathula Pass into Gangtok, Sikkim, then into India. This was a longer route compared to the one via Jelapla into Rhenock, Sikkim, to Pedong in India, then to Kalimpong. This was the main hub of the trading centre. Kalimpong was under Bhutan till 1865, so the Tibetans started trade with Bhutan long before.

The trade routes were just narrow mule tracks through extremely hazardous terrain. The hardy mules, the only means of transport, came with their untamed, ill tempered, uncouth, surly masters. These men with nerves of steel and stamina, with their beasts of burden, were the only ones, suited for this treacherous journey of three grueling weeks. Not only did they have to deal with a journey fraught with danger but had to ward off infernal bandits and diabolic weather. No ordinary traveller, not even the over enthusiastic ones, ever tried to traverse this dangerous route for fun.

In 1879, the British army sent a military expedition to Tibet. They built a road from Pedong to Jelepla Pass. Father Lesaleur of the French Mission in Pedong accompanied them as their Chaplin. The expedition didn't make much headway so they came back. The French Missionaries had stationed themselves in the farthest outpost of India, closest to Tibet, with the sole intention of entering Tibet, to preach Christianity to a totally Buddist country. This did not happen.

After the Younghusband's expedition in 1903, trade flourished and reached its peak in the 1950s in Kalimpong. This route was Kalimpong's life line, its road to glory and riches. People doing business with Tibet became rich overnight and Kalimpong became a famous trading town.

Heavily laden mule trains brought in raw untreated wool, yak tails, *churpi,* hides, Peshmina wool, borax, rock salt, musk, dried yak meat, carpets, *bakhu* material, *dhup,* medicinal herbs and gold dust. From India they carried back biscuits, maize, *papad,* flour, gun powder, cotton goods, woollen goods, matches, soap, tobacco, dried fruits, hardware, sugar, petrol and tins of *Dalda.*

The coarse raw wool which cost Rs. 40 to Rs. 60 in Tibet fetched Rs. 1400 by the time it reached Kalimpong. A huge wool *godown,* was constructed in the 10th. Mile to store the wool. It still stands to this day. When trading stopped, it was used as a college for some time.

The tins of *Dalda,* that arrived in Tibet from Kalimpong, must have been sold at a premium too. The Tibetan's insatiable demand for *Dalda,* must have been for lighting the thousands of lamps in monasteries and people's homes. The long and difficult journey was responsible for hiking up the price of every item.

The Bose family was one of the pioneers of this trade between the two countries. Marwari business men jumped in, seizing the opportunity, and became millionaires.

The routes from Chumbi Valley to Kalimpong had storage points, staging houses and transit trading centres along the way. These were necessary to relieve the hardships endured on the long hair raising journey for both men and beasts. There were no check posts, no other hindrances like passports and visas. Trade agents regulated trade. David Macdonald, the owner of Himalayan Hotel in Kalimpong, was one such agent.

Although the trade routes passed through Sikkim, not much trade took place between Tibet and Sikkim. At that time Sikkim was an autonomous country and didn't produce the tradings goods required in large quantities. Today it is a different story.

Now the muleteers and mule trains are things of the past. I remember the husky, strapping, powerful muleteers; their braided hair wound rounds their heads, a Tibetan hat with ear flaps sitting on top. They had sun tanned, leathery, flat, broad faces. They sweated profusely in their heavy woollen *Bokhus* and knee-high boots. The only weapon they carried was a long dagger, dangling from their waists. This lethal weapon was used most effectively for every possible purpose, most often, to sever the head from a body, at the drop of a hat.

I used to be frightened of these fierce men with their ferocious, black Tibetan hounds. Each the size of a small calf with jet black woolly coat. The only bit of colour on them being their bright red tongues, lolling out in the heat of a lower altitude. Man and dog walked along with the dark brown, surefooted mules weighed down with impossible loads. They walked in a single file raising dust. Each animal sported a big bell. Their jingling bells were neither sharp nor loud but produced a dull, soothing, lilting music. Each bell rang separately but produced a harmony of lows and highs depending on the speed of the mules. These bells were attached to the mules so that their masters could find them easily if they strayed or got lost.

If I was frightened of these muleteers, my uncle was terrified of them. Just one encounter with a muleteer forced him to give them a very wide berth!

Every year, in the month of March, the Pedong *mela,* was organized by the agriculture Department of West Bengal in Pedong. My uncle was the Director of that department so had to make several trips to Pedong during the *mela.* He stayed in Monjula with us in Kalimpong each time. His means of transport was an old American weapon's carrier. Large enough to contain all at Monjula plus friends who wanted to attend the *mela.*

The huge hulk of a truck rattled down the uneven, unpaved, narrow road to Algarah, threatening to break every bone in our bodies. All the noises it made were far louder than its rather faint horn. We had to leave the truck behind at Algarah as the motor able road ended there. The next four miles to Pedong had to be done on foot through dense, dark forests.

Every time we drove to Algarah in uncle's truck, we would invariably come across a muleteer with his mule train, on this stretch of road, being the last leg of the trade route to Kalimpong.

The shy mules, creatures of the wild, were not used to cars, leave alone a huge dark monster of a truck, thundering down on them, spouting strange noises, threatening to swallow them up. Eyes stark with fright, the terrified mules would run for their dear lives, scattering all over the hill sides. The muleteer had no end of trouble, to bring back his herd on the road again. This always proved to be a difficult proposition, mules being the stubbornness of animals.

One day a tired and disgruntled muleteer, after his strenuous long journey, was infuriated by the intrusion of uncle's monster of a truck causing havoc to his mule train. He drew out his dagger, eyes blazing, came charging behind the truck to slaughter us all. Luckily, our truck picked up speed, to leave the heavily clad muleteer in his cumbersome garb far behind.

Uncle, S.P. Bose, was so shaken up by this incident that whenever he saw the slightest wisp of dust in the distance, long before he saw or heard the mules, he would ask his driver to stop dead in his tracks until the mule train had passed by.

The mule train would be parked outside Kalimpong town where the mules would be relieved of their burden for a few days. To relax and ruminate till the next lot of heavy bags and boxes were loaded and strapped on their backs again.

The huge wooden boxes, encased in hide, with strips of metal for decoration and crude clasps were not as strong as steel trunks but served the purpose of carrying delicate goods intact. I still have such a box, an antique now.

The muleteers were men of few words. They didn't socialize with the people of Kalimpong. They kept to themselves. They had a job in hand and took their work seriously.

They often encountered the most unlikely of visitors in the 1950s, Prince Peter of Greece and Denmark. An anthropologist by profession. He was very comfortably settled in Kalimpong. He always arrived at the muleteer's camp whenever he heard of the new arrival of a mule train from Tibet.

He made it his business to carry on his anthropological research on these men straight from Tibet. A pure breed. He measured their skulls, bones etc. He had picked up enough Tibetan to converse with these simple people. The rumour was that the Prince was a spy and his only interest was to glean information out of them about the situation in Tibet.

The Chinese invasion, oppression and occupation of Tibet were in full swing. The muleteers were the only people coming out of Tibet, the forbidden land wrapped in mystery. They were the only source of information about the situation in Tibet.

As the Chinese invasion cast a determined stranglehold on Tibet, the VIPs and many rich Tibetans fled from Tibet using the trade route to Kalimpong. This trade route proved to be the golden route to liberty. The trade route faltered and completely stopped by 1960. This closure of the trade route saw the demise of Kalimpong from a very important and prosperous trading town, throbbing with activity, to a dead one.

Over the years, as bitter relations prevailed between India and China, we were hopeful, living in a Communist State, that our communist Chief Minister, Mr. Jyoti Basu, would take the initiative to reopen the trade route once more. It would not only benefit Kalimpong but the pitifully poor state of West Bengal as well.

The pipe dream of the people of Kalimpong never happened. We lived with this dream for 40 long years. Now it is shattered once and for all.

Sikkim, the favoured state of the Indian Government, has bagged this trade route. This new trade route will be a piece of cake. Wide metalled roads, from both countries, will meet at Nathula. Big trucks will roll in and out easily making trade fast, furious and easy.

The charm of that special breed of colourful, swashbuckling muleteers with their dogs and mules with their sweet sounding bells, will never come to Kalimpong again.

Pedong Mela

The agricultural *Mela,* held once a year, in the month of March in Pedong, was a great attraction for us, children, staying in Kalimpong. It was an occasion we looked forward to liven up our uncluttered, simple existence devoid of T.V. and Bollywood.

My uncle, Mr. S.P. Bose Director of agriculture and Dr. Robi Som, went to great lengths to make this *mela* a success for the villagers of the small, sleepy town of Pedong. This *mela* was held to encourage the farmers to produce more and better crops, vegetables, dairy products, farm animals and poultry. The agriculture department was always providing aid and know how to these farmers. The *mela* was an opportunity for them to display their produce and livestock also.

Pedong just twenty miles away from Kalimpong seemed like a hundred miles to us. This journey would take us almost four hours to complete. We would clatter down the narrow bumpy, unmetalled, road in uncle's enormous weapon's carrier. A rattle trap, discarded by the American G.I.S but sturdy and strong, impregnable as a tank. We would pile into the spacious rear, singing to our heart's content, under a clear blue sky, without the suffocating canvas hood, on top, to block our view or dampen our spirits.

There was not much traffic on the road except for the swarthy muleteer steering his mule train down to Kalimpong or on his way to Tibet. The dumb mules would walk obediently in a single file, carrying back breaking loads, raising clouds of dust. Swirling dust that settled on our hair turning it yellow or orange akin to today's expensive fad but totally free for us. Being covered in a film of dust, breathing it, tasting the grit in our mouths only added fun and flavour to our adventure.

No traffic therefore, no traffic rules to follow on this road but we had to give way to every mule train we came across or face unpleasant consequences. The wrath of the enraged muleteer was to be avoided at any cost. The usually docile mules would take flight at the sight and sound of our rattling truck. They would break ranks, career down the hillsides in terror, often dislodging their precious cargo down a *jhora.* To maintain order was a huge task for the muleteer. His first reaction would be to draw out his sharp long dagger and charge at the object that was responsible for his woe. Our truck!

Completely unprotected at the back of the truck, we would be cowering and squealing with fear as the muleteer, transformed into a raging demon came charging down at us. His long pigtail flying behind him, layers and layers of his cumbersome clothes flapping, eyes flaming, face contorted with rage, mouthing death and damnation, his long, razor sharp dagger glinting in the sunlight, was enough to give us heart attacks! To avoid this murderous onslaught our truck always stopped to let the mule train pass. We would sit stiffly not daring to whisper or breathe until the coast was clear.

Our adventures did not end at Algarah where the dusty, apology of a motor able road ended. The next four miles to Pedong entailed a journey on foot through a forest of tall trees on a strip of a moss covered, slippery path. This part of the journey I loved most of all. I loved tripping down this deep, dense forest, leaping over crystal clear bubbling, gurgling little mountain *jhoras.* We would all stop at the first *jhora* we came across to dip our feet in the cool, cool water and wash off the layers of powdery dust from our faces and hair.

The forest floor damp and green never saw the rays of the sun through the thick canopy of trees. The birds disturbed by our rude intrusion into their private territory would squeak and send alarm signals warning their flocks. The woodpecker, not in the least bothered by our presence, would carry on tap tapping the on tree nonchalantly. The squirrels would scamper to the safety of the highest branch and turn their beady eyes to watch our movements anxiously. The drone of wasps and the crickets orchestra filled the forest air.

The forest would end abruptly and we would be right in front of the *mela*, ground. A flat grass covered piece of land as big as a football field. Just above the *mela* ground stood the old British dak bungalow where we would spend the night. We enjoyed those fun filled, lantern-lit nights, listening to frightening ghost stories. We were sure the dak bungalow was haunted and huddled together to avoid an encounter with any Englishman who might appear to claim his residence from us.

I remember an amusing incident in the dak bungalow once. Mr. Moti Chand Pradhan, the SDO of Kalimpong, with his family had accompanied us to the dak bungalow. His two children Ajali and Chandrajyoti were my good friends. Sunkumari *didi* and Mulukchand were also there with us.

As usual we clung to each other in the dimly lit bedroom listening to ghost stories, when I noticed a white shape at the window. I was petrified with fright. The others, noticing my colourless, terror stricken face looking at the window, turned their gaze towards it. There was pin drop silence in the room as they too stared at the white blob outside through the window pane.

"The Englishman!" somebody whispered. "No, don't be silly, all the Englishmen are gone forever!" "Let's open the window and see," whispered someone. At this juncture ma appeared. "What is the matter?" She asked alarmed by the look on our faces. "There is a ghost out there," I stuttered, pointing to the window. "Rubbish!" she exclaimed. She rushed to the window flung it wide open, looked out and started laughing. "There is your ghost!" she laughed pointing at a stray cow which had got its horns hopelessly entangled in a white sheet drying on the line outside.

From the dark bungalow the small *mela* ground, down below, presented a scene of much activity. Long stalls were set up with thatched roofs for displaying agricultural produce, farm animals and poultry. The villagers brought their best vegetables, hens, eggs, goats and cattle. There were ribbons and cash prizes to be won in each category. Fat, healthy livestock and enormous vegetables would be displayed proudly by the Bhutia and Lepcha farmers of the area.

Once I took the largest eggs, laid by my hens, to exhibit at the *mela.* There was a very interesting weighing machine for grading the eggs, according to size and weight. I was fascinated as each egg rolled down a narrow steel channel and gently dropped into a compartment below. As soon as it's landed its correct weight was determined by the machine. The heavier the egg, the sooner the base of the channel parted to allow it to fall, the lighter the egg the longer its journey down the channel. I was delighted when I won the second prize for my eggs! I received a ribbon and Rs. 2 as my prize!

The *mela* was usually opened by somebody from Kalimpong. Once the Agriculture Minister, Dr. R. Ahmed, a very good friend of baba's, arrived all the way from Kolkata to open the *mela*. He stayed with us at Monjula and then made the long trek to Pedong. He was provided with a horse for the last leg of the journey to save him from walking. He took one look at the emaciated, miserable horse and decided to walk instead. This was the solitary horse of the area that was always produced to carry the young and the ailing if the need arose.

The villagers of Pedong were highly excited at the prospect of a Minister coming to open their *mela*. It was a simple affair usually with a handful of people attending the ceremony but this time people from far and wide came to see the Minister from Calcutta. They went away very disappointed. They had expected to see a handsome man, dressed in his finery of medals and plumes riding on a super white steed, perhaps with wings attached too! Dr. R. Ahmed on the other hand was a simple, short, dark man with no hair to boast of, clad in a drab grey safari suit.

It was great fun going around the *mela* even though there were no junk and trinket stalls. We were quite happy to admire the animals, poultry and vegetables.

One year a small circus company had braved the difficult road and landed at the *mela* ground. The much patched, faded tent with gaping holes did not deter the villagers from thronging to see the circus. They happily sat on the carpet of green grass, watched the acrobats and a couple of ragged clown at their antics which sent the villagers into gales of uncontrollable laughter. They watched mesmerized as they had never been to a circus before. It was great entertainment being dished out to them for the first time.

The cows and bulls to be judged were paraded on the grounds like race horses. The proud owners struggled, pushing, pulling, coercing the lazy animals to a faster trot, to wipe off their stupid bovine smiles and look more animated and intelligent. They never succeeded to do so.

The baby show was another great attraction of the *mela*. The young Bhutia and Lepcha mothers arrived with their well fed babies slung on their backs. Ma and other ladies of Kalimpong were always requested to judge this show. There was no weighing scales or any other method used for judging the babies. The judges had to depend solely on their eyes to pick out the healthiest baby in each category.

The babies safely ensconced on their mother's comfortable laps, did not object to being inspected by the prying eyes of the judges. If a sensitive, shy baby took offence at being stared at by complete strangers, she would let out a loud howl, to be shut up at once with the mother's nipple stuffed into her wide open mouth.

The weather during March is always bright and sunny except for one year when a dreadful thunder storm appeared out of the blue. It was the last day of the *mela* and we were on our way home. We were not prepared for such a down pour. Ma at once asked for the sole horse, of skin and bones, to save me from walking the four miles to Algarah in pouring rain.

My cousin, Bunty a healthy, strong, lazy young man seizing the opportunity, jumped on the saddle behind me. Although he was extremely thin, his weight, added to my slight one, must have been enough to cave in the poor horse's vertebrae until it touched his innards. We looked a sorry sight perched up on the lethargic horse. Me crouching in front while my cousin Bunty's long legs almost touching the ground.

We entered the thick forest. It was like a boiling cauldron. The tree tops waved their heads in frenzy in the wind that threatened to lop them off. Florescent white streaks of lightning lit the dark forest at regular intervals. The deafening thunder claps rent the air. Huge branches came crashing down all around us, missing us by inches. Smaller branches popped sharply like pistol shots. Rain pelted down on the trees showering us with cascading leaves. I clung to the saddle terrified.

No amount of whipping or rib prodding could make our horse move faster. He trotted on at snail's pace unperturbed by the havoc the electric storm was creating. He seemed to know his way so he plodded on unconcerned. Bunty held the reins and his large raincoat covered us. My exposed hands were stiff with cold. Just as abruptly as it had arrived the storm departed to let loose its fury on other unsuspecting mortals. The forest was pitch dark now.

At last we saw the outline of the rows of houses in Algarah. Here too darkness prevailed. I was stiff as a board with cold. My brain had become numb too. We went down the road to the last house where we had been asked to wait for the others.

When we reached the small hut, Bunty got off the horse and knocked on the door. An old lady came out with a lantern. The docile unfazed horse's eyes dilated, he shied and took off, down the steep road, in a gallop. His eyes had got used to the dark; the sudden flash of light unnerved and frightened him out of his apathy. He took off in sheer desperation.

I clung to the saddle. My hands were too stiff with cold to grab the reins. I was an expert equestrian but now I was helplessly clinging to the saddle for dear life. The horse ran at the very edge of the road. There were no houses on this slope that plunged steeply to kingdom come. There was every chance that both of us would go rolling down. The only thing left for me to do, to save myself, was to deliberately fall off the saddle on to the road. This I did and lay in a heap. The horse disappeared in the darkness.

Bunty came running helter skelter, picked me up and carried me into the hut. He was mad with worry. He kept asking me if I was hurt. He was sure I had a few broken bones. He knew ma would kill him if any such thing happened to me. I was so cold, my teeth were chattering and I couldn't speak. At last I formed the words, "I am not hurt only frozen." Bunty heaved a huge sigh of relief. He still remembers those words and says they are the sweetest words he had ever heard.

Burma Raja

He was well known in Kalimpong as the Burma *Raja,* he was not a *raja* at all but had the life style of a *Maharaja* and temperament to match.

King Thibaw of Burma and his family were exiled by the British in India at Ratnagiri. The king had handpicked the second son of his Field Marshal Duke and Duchess of Ngaphe and Mindat of Burma, Mr. Kim Mong Latthakin, to marry his second daughter, crown Princess Ashin Teiksu Myat Paye Latt. Lord Willingdon and Mr. Smith, the Collector of Ratnagiri, were witnesses to this marriage in 1917.

If history had taken its natural course, the second princess would have been the queen of Burma after King Thibaw's death. King Thibaw with that in mind had chosen the fiery, dynamic, smart, well-educated young man, of royal blood to be her consort, fit and capable of ruling Burma one day. Unfortunately this never happened; the couple lived and died in Kalimpong never to see their beloved country again.

After the wedding they were allowed to leave Ratnagiri and live in Calcutta for three years at 22, Mcleod Street. They were given an option to go to Tibet but they decided to leave Calcutta and live in Kalimpong, so they arrived here in 1920. They were put up at the old P.W.D. Bungalow by the British S.D.O. They lived there for two years. The S.D.O. Mr. Goode offered them Rs. 10,000 from his coffers in exchange of a receipt but the *Raja* refused. He put them up in Springburn, now Basic Training College. In January 1934 there was an earthquake and Springburn was badly damaged.

The *Raja* wrote to the British Government for two lacs to buy land and build a house. The money was sanctioned but disappeared mysteriously.

In 1935 The *Raja* wrote to the Government again to send the promised money or buy Springburn for them. There was no reply so as an act of defiance; he refused to renew his gun licenses. This turned out to be a grave error. In 1937 they shifted to Arcadia and eventually to Tapoban on Upper Cart Road and lived here for many years. The Government paid Rs.100 per month for Tapoban.

What annoyed the *Raja* most was the reduction of the *Rani's* pension from Rs. 1000 per month to Rs. 300 only. He refused to accept this meager sum but without his knowledge the *Rani* kept on accepting it.

His sole occupation became writing letters to all British officers from Lord Willingdon downwards. In one letter he said that his wife, who was from the first family of Burma, was getting less pension than lesser Burmese officers of the King. In fact she should be the Queen of England.

Before they left Ratnagiri Lord Willingdon through Mr. J. P. Brander had told them that the British Government would sell all King Thibaw's private properties including the palace in Mandalay and give them the money to live on. This was a second hand verbal message nothing in writing which the *Raja* was convinced the British would honour, being an honorable man himself but it never materialized either.

The Raja then asked the British Government to give him only Rs.15 *lacs* considering that they had stolen all king Thibaw's arms, ammunition, his palace at Mandalay with all its expensive contents, all his crown jewels, eleven life size statues of Kings of Burma cast in solid gold, all the mines and minerals of Burma, the proceeds of the palace at Ratnagiri and most important of all they had robbed them off their youth. The Government ignored the Raja's demands.

Apart from writing letters to the British, he indulged in his hobbies which included playing tennis on the clay court, he had built in Tapoban, hunting, fishing and painting. He excelled at all these. He and the *Rani*, gave lavish tea, lunch and dinner parties to their friends in Kalimpong.

These parties were strictly for adults. Ma was invited several times but I, a child, was not invited. The first time ma attended such a party she came back starry eyed. The opulence of the house, the gracious hospitality of the *Raja* and *Rani*, delicious food cooked to perfection by experienced cooks, served by liveried bearers on a table laid with exquisite china and silver cutlery. The Burmese do not use chopsticks.

After the sumptuous meal a silver finger bowl was placed in front of each guest. When ma dipped her fingers into the sweet scented warm water, she touched something hard at the bottom of the bowl. Intrigued she peered into the bowl, six large, perfect, pigeon blood rubies winked back at her; "why didn't you bring them home?" I gasped. "They were only on display dear, not a present."

Every evening the Raja played tennis on his private tennis court with his friends. Tea was served at the tennis court which consisted of wafer thin cucumber sandwiches, cake and pastry in true British style. Silver jugs of cold lemonade for the very thirsty.

The *Raja* loved to hunt, for this purpose he had five excellent guns and rifles tailor made to his specifications. Lord Willingdon, the viceroy of India, had once proposed to give a small part of a forest to the Raja for his private use. The

Raja declined, he preferred to be free to shoot anywhere he liked. He wrote to Willingdon, "As a sportsman I will naturally abide by all the rules regarding off season and other customary observances of *Shikar,* hunting. This is essential to maintain my health and peace of mind." He went on to say that game was scarce in India because of foreigners (British) who indiscriminately shot everything in sight.

I clearly remember hearing about one hunting expedition of his which caused quite a commotion in Kalimpong. The hunting party had consisted of the *Raja,* his friends, the beaters and a high ranking Indian official of the British Government. The hunters formed a wide semi-circle beating, whatever they carried, to frighten the animals and drive them towards the hunters ready with their guns. The trigger happy officer noticed a deer, aimed and shot at it. The cry that rent the air was not that of a wounded deer but of a mortally wounded young beater.

Unfortunately the young boy was wearing a brown shirt which resembled a deer's colouring through the thick undergrowth.

The *Raja* had refused to renew his gun licenses when the *Rani's* pension had been reduced. He hunted for one year without any license but as an act of defiance he informed the local S.D.O. About it. The S.D.O. Mr. Stacy, called on the *Raja* in 1936 and told him not to bother about renewing gun licenses as he was not a terrorist and wouldn't misuse his guns. The *Raja* admired the wisdom of the British Government. But not for long.

In 1936 Mr. Crassby, D.S.P. Of Darjeeling, arrived unexpectedly at the Raja's house. He forced his way into the drawing room and very rudely demanded to see his gun licenses. The *Raja,* flatly refused. The Raja told him that he had no business to come to his house without prior permission and information. He sent him packing. This turned out to be a fatal mistake.

Early morning on 17th. January 1937, the S.D.O. Mr. Seth Druquor, arrived at Acadia, the *Raja's* residence then, with a posse of twelve policemen with strict verbal instructions from the Deputy Commissioner, to confiscate the *Raja's* guns. They would all be dismissed from their services if they did not. The *Raj*a refused to part with his guns and showed them copies of letters he had written to the Government.

The S.D.O. and police officers entreated him to part with his guns but he was adamant. In desperation the police inspector and the O.C. offered themselves to be shot and killed by the *Raja.* They said they would rather choose death than be dismissed from their services as their wives and children would starve.

Finally, the Raja was moved by the thought of starving wives, children and of killing in cold blood agreed to part with his guns, on conditions that they were broken into small pieces in front of him. Mr. Drukuor did this job well and carried away those beloved, priceless guns of the *Raja's* away in pieces.

He wrote to the Government immediately saying, "I could not allow them to take my guns intact, as it is contrary to my code of honour, for which I had then decided to put up a fight to the end. In order to save bloodshed I consented to their breaking my guns before taking them away. It was an act of absolute mischief and jealousy and I loath to go into details." He asked for Rs. 20,000 as compensation for his guns. He goes on to mention Mr. Crassby D.S.P., "We have forgotten and forgiven him. Now we are told that he is one of the principally responsible men for the above black hearted act."

The British lied to the *Raja* continuously then did everything possible to harass, bind, gag and bring this impossible man to his knees. The *Raja* now bereft of his guns, took up his pen to demand his heritage and ridicule them. A brave and gallant man he took every opportunity to puncture the British ego.

In 1928 the local English daily of Burma Sun, carried this heading, "Burmese Prince's unique challenge to ex-Governor, Sir Harcourt Butler." The Prince had written a letter to the viceroy to allow Queen Supayalat's cremation or alternately requested his Excellency's permission to fight a duel with Harcourt Butler, the Ex-Governor of Burma, against whom the Prince had a number of grievances. Not only did the Prince request him for the sanction of the duel but also asked him to discharge the function of an umpire.

The *Raja,* apart from being good at outdoor activities, was an excellent artist. I have seen some of his paintings still in existence. He painted nature dramatically and beautifully. One painting still hangs in Topoban where he lived for sixteen years. Age has not deteriorated the vibrant colours.

The Burmese Princess was known as *Rani Sahib,* in Kalimpong. She was diametrically opposite of her husband, the *Raja.* A tiny, sweet, gentle, soft spoken lady was not interested in any of his activities. Her only interest in life was her adopted Nepali son, Mouluji affectionately called Alooji. She loved, pampered and spoilt him to distraction. He was brought up like a Prince.

He was admitted to St. Joseph's Convent. He went back and forth from school on horseback. The *sais* and a bearer accompanied him. The bearer's duty was to sit outside, near the classroom window, so Alooji would feel reassured to see him at hand and also take him to the toilet when necessary. At lunch time, another bearer would come loaded with crockery, cutlery and a tiffin carrier full of his favourite food.

When India got her independence the British departed without making any provision for the *Raja* and *Rani,* leaving them at the mercy of the new Indian Government. The *Rani's* pension was depleted further and the house rent of Rs.100 stopped. The Raja was not prepared to give up his life style so the *Rani* quietly, with the help of a faithful servant, started selling her Jewellery and valuables one by one for a pittance, until nothing was left.

Eventually in 1953, they were forced to shift to a smaller, cheaper two bed-roomed house, Panaroma ii, right next door to our house, Monjula. Alooji, a few years older than me came down to play on our big lawn every evening. We became good friends and still are.

The Raja now, could not indulge in any of his pastimes but he never gave up smoking his aromatic Burma *cheroots.* He was getting older, frailer and mellower by the day but his courage and pride never deserted him.

From my bedroom window I would watch him walking up and down the little footpath in front of his house in his white turban. Sitting in the small gazebo, listening to the tinkling of the tiny bells, attached to the conical brass five feet high structure, sitting on the roof of the gazebo. This was brought all the way from Burma. It is called 'Khanug lung,' in the Burmese language which means bell and they adorn the top of some pagodas in Burma. This bell still sits atop the Gazebo in Panaroma ii.

The *Raja* once owned a highly pedigreed pair of Grey hounds, mongrels now replaced them. One such dog always played havoc in our compound, chasing, killing our chickens and stealing food from our kitchen. One evening, determined to scare this mongrel, I waited behind a bush with my small, powerless air gun. Soon the dog approached. As he was passing me, I pumped in a tiny pellet at point blank range into his side. The dog did not give a yelp of pain but ran straight back to his house and then to every one's surprise dropped dead.

That evening Alooji came to call me to his house for the first time. "My father wants to see you and your gun," he said. Quaking in my shoes, I went to meet the *Raja* with my air gun. He was surely going to scold me for killing his dog. He was smoking his *cherrot* when I entered. "I am sorry I killed your dog, I only wanted to scare him but he died." I finished off lamely with my head down. "Well done," he said. "Now let me see your gun." I handed the air gun to him. He inspected it, gently ran his frail fingers over the slim barrel caressing it lovingly.

His thoughts must have gone back to those powerful, wonderful guns that he was once the proud owner. "How did you manage to kill a dog with such a light gun?" he asked. I didn't have the answer till the next day when it was discovered that the little pellet had perforated the dog's heart.

His speech was guttural with a heavy Burmese accent and his short sentences or words seemed to get lost in his grey moustache, I found it very difficult to understand his speech.

That was my first face to face encounter with the Raja but not the last. He asked me to come again and I did, very often in fact. He would tell me the most fascinating true stories about his past, his country but his favourite stories were about King Thibaw and his family and what the British did to them. He now lived totally in the past. He found a very interested and good listener in me.

I was just a young teenager who shared his interests. I loved guns and tennis. As soon as he heard that I had taken up tennis, he gave me all his racquets. They were really old fashioned and I never used them. I wish I had kept them; they would be antiques of great value now. I took up painting much later but I could never be as good as he was.

He told me how in 1886 when Burma was annexed, King Thibaw with his two queens and two daughters were captured by General Sladen at their palace in Mandalay. They were put in the steamer Suria to be exiled in India. King Thibaw was told by the British that they were being taken to India for negotiations, temporarily and not for good.

During the voyage General Sladen asked the King to show him the famous, in-valuable ruby set on his ring known as nga Mauk ruby. Sladen pocketed the ring and told the King that all his valuable jewellery should be kept in the ship's safe. He would hand them back on reaching their destination. The king believed him and gave him everything for safe keeping. Sladen went down the steamer and was never seen again by the king.

When King George V of England came to India for his coronation in 1911, the King wrote giving a list and asked for his private jewellery to be returned. The Government wrote back to say General Sladen was dead and there was no trace of the Jewellery yet, the eleventh edition of encyclopedia Britannica Volume IV page 846 to 848 mentions part of the looted property with their values. I wonder where the ruby ring is, it must be worth a fortune.

The Raja mentioned that Queen Victoria was very annoyed with Lord Dufferin for capturing the friendly King of Burma and annexing Burma without her knowledge but later Lord Dufferin was given the title of Lord Dufferin of Ava, the name of the old capital of Burma.

There was a letter written to King Thibaw by Her Majesty of the United Kingdom of Great Britain and Ireland and empress of India to condole the death of his father King Mindon. It was signed "I am your Majesty's sincere friend and well-wisher, Victoria R.1." This letter is priceless but missing.

The *Raja* and *Rani* had been reduced to abject poverty. One day the *Rani's* faithful maid came to ma with two thick silk *lungis.* The *Rani* had sent them to ma in lieu of Rs. 40. Ma sent the *lungis,* and Rs. 40. back to her.

Financial decline and failing health took their toll. The lion hearted, noble man who was to become the prince consort to the queen of Burma died a pauper in Kalimpong. The *Rani* went to Calcutta and died soon after.

In 2000 I visited Burma now, Myanmar. I asked many people about their royal family but no one remembered them. They remember king Thibaw vaguely. They had no idea what became of him and his family.

I visited Mandalay and as I stood on Mandalay hill and looked down, I could clearly see the huge rectangle, well preserved palace walls with a wide moat all around. There is no palace there anymore but a green field and army barracks. I went back to my childhood and visualized the palace as it was with all its pomp, grandeur and glory. Once more I could distinctly hear the *Raja's* voice whispering in my ear, the tales of that glorious era.

Jamai Babu

At the ripe old age of seventy he looked every inch the *Jamai* as he was on the day of his wedding. Apart from his looks, life style and dress code which proclaimed him as a *jamai* babu, his status in Kalimpong was of a *Jamai* being the husband of Leela Bose, daughter of Kalimpong.

Leela Bose was the owner of the most renowned business house in Kalimpong Leela Bose and Company. Kalimpong was quick to lay claim to the prosperous lady from Calcutta as its very own daughter. He was her consort, therefore, became the son- in-law. A role he reveled in and fulfilled to the hilt, playing it effortlessly, proudly and happily.

Jatin Babu, as he was called, in his youth was a very successful business man of Calcutta and had amassed great wealth. He imported motor cars from England and sold them to the rich and the powerful. He constantly came in contact with *rajas* and *maharajas* who ordered their cars from him. He developed princely tastes and habits in the process.

Once, when holidaying in Darjeeling, the playground of the rich, he took a fancy to the blue domed Burdhman mansion there and decided to buy it. He paid the earnest money for it in gold *mohors* but the transaction fell through.

During this very holiday, being an adventurous, energetic young man he made a trip to Kalimpong on horseback as there were no proper roads then, connecting the two towns. He fell in love with Kalimpong. He had no plans of settling there until disaster struck. The ship carrying his consignment of expensive motor cars and bicycles from England sank in mid ocean. This stupendous loss along with many a shylock demanding his 'pound of flesh,' completely demoralized nd devastated him. He developed a great distaste and abhorrence for any kind of business for the rest of his life.

Depressed and distressed, he gave up the bright lights of Calcutta and arrived in Kalimpong with his wife Leela and five children. He took up residence in a flat in Kanchanjungha *Kothi,* then shifted to Dilkhusha a large house nearby, to accommodate his large family. In 1920 he purchased a big tract of prime land on Upper Cart road and set about building Topoban.

The house took two years to build. Every item for its construction came from Calcutta by train to Siliguri, from there by bullock cart through unchartered terrain on an apology of a road, to Kalimpong.

Once ready, he did not retire into seclusion of his idyllic retreat of meditation, Topaban, instead, he rented it out to the so called Burmese Prince for a number of years. He moved in eventually.

Leela Bose, a tiny little gutsy woman with tremendous business acumen but no prior experience, launched into business with her two young sons. Thus Leela Bose and Company was born.

To start with, they opened a department store, the first and last of its kind in Kalimpong. It was a thundering success. The small stores in town with meager stocks and limited variety were soon over taken by this well stocked store which carried all essentials of daily life, from readymadc garments to dolls. Next L. Bose and Company started trade with Tibet. Never short of novel ideas, they started a gramophone store in the premises where Adarsh Medicine store stands now. Then the Novelty Cinema. It was originally housed in a large tin shed with wooden benches just below the *Mela* ground. This is where I got my first taste of Hollywood and its stars. L. Bose and Company became a household name. They were the pioneers of business in Kalimpong.

Jatin Babu shunned all business; was happy and content to lead a life of leisure, indulging in his one and only favourite pastime, eating good food. He lived to eat.

A connoisseur of food he was invited to every party at our house, Monjula, not only to give his expert opinion on every dish prepared but the way he did justice to the food with great enjoyment and relish, it was ma's reward for a perfectly cooked meal.

All delicacies Baba brought from Calcutta were equally divided and distributed to 'delicacy' starved neighbours. The first portion always went to Jatin Babu the connoisseur. *Misti doi, khajur gur,* canned food and *elish mach* arrived regularly. I used to be fascinated by solid pieces of choicest *elish mach,* shining with oil, coming out of an enormous earthen pot. With no ice boxes around, baba would bring cleaned, sliced *elish*, perfectly preserved, in an earthen pot of mustard oil.

Every morning, Jatin Babu would visit neighbours to while away the hours. Monjula, happened to be his regular port of call. He would appear impeccably dressed in his spotless white *dhuti* and *punjabi.* A neatly folded cotton shawl on his left shoulder, highly polished black pumps, 24 carat gold rimmed spectacles and a silver knobbed cane completing the picture of a perfect, aristocratic Bengali *Jamai babu.*

A strand of his thick silver hair refused to conform to the strictness of the comb, lay curled rakishly on his broad forehead giving him a boyish look. An ample white moustache flared above his ruddy round cheeks. His parted lips displayed a perfect set of strong white teeth, all his own, worn by years of mastication but still fit enough to demolish ample quantities of food.

The appearance of this garrulous old man on the garden path of Monjula would send all the adults scampering to various superfluous occupations. I would be the only one to greet him happily at the door. His round jovial face would light up when he saw me. We would sit on the verandah talking for hours, occasionally interrupted by adults who arrived, in turn, to inquire after his health politely with much concern then, disappeared fast, mumbling excuses about very pressing unfinished work.

Jatin Babu was seventy and I was seven but we were the best of friends. The common bond between us being pork. We both loved it. I was a very poor and fussy eater, had no interest in food except for pork.

During my seven years I must have tasted ham, bacon and sausages just about a dozen times, out of cans, brought from the British army canteen by baba, another pork lover. On the other hand my old friend must have devoured herds of pigs during his seventy years.

Fresh pork was never prepared in 'Monjula.' Ma maintained that pigs were ugly, germ ridden, filthy animals and their detestable meat most unhygienic. In short, sheer poison.

Jatin Babu, well aware of ma's aversion to pork and my limited exposure to it, tried to make up for it by educating me and keeping my taste buds alive for the king of all meats, pork. He would give detailed descriptions of the most delectable, scrumptious pork dishes until oodles of salvia flooded my mouth. "The most delicious dish in the world is pork roast." He proclaimed.

"Do you know how roasted pork was discovered?" he would ask me. I had heard this story innumerable times but it never failed to excite and thrill me so, I would shake my head vigorously and say "No, please tell me." With every repetition the embellishments increased.

Settling down more comfortably on the wicker chair, his eyes twinkling, he would start this story and I would listen wide eyed. "Long, long ago, a prisoner was brought before the king of Siam for trial. His crime was arson. He regularly set fire to people's pig sties killing all the pigs. He gave no reason for his behaviour nor tried to defend himself when apprehended and thrown into jail. On hearing the details of this monstrous case the king ordered death by hanging. As was the custom, the king asked him if he had a last wish. "Yes Sire" the prisoner answered eagerly, "I will die a happy man if I can taste roasted pig's meat for the last time." The king was shocked at this despicable request; shock waves ran through the whole court. Pig's meat was strictly taboo in Siam; anyone found eating it was put to death immediately without a trial. "Let us hang him at once," cried the people, enraged. The king was intrigued and wanted to know the reason behind the prisoner's strange request.

"Sire, many years ago," began the prisoner, "During my travels I came across a village which had been completely gutted. There was not a soul anywhere. I was tired and very hungry so I poked around the remains of a house hoping to find some unburnt morsel of food to eat but everything had been burnt to cinders. I was walking away in despair when I spotted the carcass of a pig burnt golden brown, amongst the dying embers. Throwing taboos to the wind, I cut a small piece of the golden flesh and put it into my mouth. It was delicious! I had never tasted anything like it, so once back home, I deliberately set fire to people's livestock and quietly gorged myself on roasted pigs that died in the fire."

The king, amazed by this bizarre story, got his cooks to roast a pig for the prisoner to fulfill his last request. Cooked to perfection, choicest and most appetizing, soft, succulent pieces of golden brown roast pork arrived for the condemned man.

The king watched with growing interest as the prisoner devoured the pieces with utmost relish smacking his lips and licking his fingers. He couldn't resist the temptation of trying one piece. A look of wonder and delight appeared on his royal face. "This is marvelous!" he shouted, "I have never tasted anything like it!" The king was so pleased with this delicious discovery that he not only pardoned the prisoner but made him the chief cook of his palace, a coveted and prestigious position. He also declared that anyone of his subjects, who did not partake of this delicious meat Pork, would be put to death.

This was a wonderful story, I loved it specially the way it was told and enacted. My only regret is, now that I am an expert at making pork roast exactly like the one Jatin Babu used to describe, he is not here to taste and enjoy it.

The grand old man was always in the pink of health due to a carefree life, tons of good rich food with no signs of such unknown diseases as blood sugar, blood pressure, or cholesterol, carried on enjoying life. Ma was therefore, surprised when she was asked by Dr. Boral to go and look after Jatin babu who had suddenly fallen ill. His whole family had left for Calcutta that winter. He had refused to go.

Ma arrived in Topoban, to find the old man in bed, sinking fast. His fat rosy cheeks sallow, his bright eyes dim, his shiny locks mat and stringy. He asked ma to chant the *Gita,* in a hoarse whisper. He had dozed off, lulled by her chanting but suddenly, woke up with a start, gathering all his energy and haltingly spoke to ma, "Charu, go to my chest of drawers over there, open the last drawer, right at the back, behind all the clothes, you will find something I have saved up for a long time for your little daughter. Please give it to her."

Ma started her search immediately with visions of gold jewellery, precious objects which the old man must have carefully laid aside for his beloved little companion, me. She searched and searched but couldn't find any velvet boxes of jewellery, the only thing she found, kept very safely hidden for me, was a can of Pork Sausages!

Tea Ceremony

Everybody in Kalimpong knew him as Khokababu. The slim, short, bespectacled, sharp featured man sporting a white *dhuti*, in summer and in the midst of severe winters, a long, cotton shirt instead of the usual *panjabi*. Fashions changed, people took to trousers but not Khokababu.

The concessions he made to ward off the cold was to wear a coat, long woollen stockings and highly polished, brown leather shoes.

He always carried a neatly rolled, long, black umbrella. This served as a walking stick rather than a protection from the sun or rain but his trade mark was his six celled torch. This he carried to work every evening.

This torch fascinated me. No one I knew owned such a marvelous torch. Its very length was incredible, it was as long as my arm. Sleek and shining, a thing of beauty. When switched on, its powerful beam could pick out objects clearly a hundred feet away.

A ray of sunlight trapped in this metal case to be used at will to penetrate the darkest corners of the night. I longed to handle it, play with it, focus it on invisible objects in the dark and see them light up and come to life. To my great disappointment it was taboo for little children.

I was a spoilt child and always got what I wanted but in spite of all my pouts and tears, I never got a chance to handle this wonderful torch. Khokababu gently, kindly but firmly explained to me that it was not a toy but a vital instrument of his profession. His profession was to run the Novelty Cinema Hall which he owned. He had to use it when the lights suddenly failed in the cinema hall and to find his way back home at midnight after the last show. It was his most useful and dependable companion. It could also be used as a weapon in case he was attacked as he made his way home alone every night.

Kalimpong was absolutely safe in those days and Khokababu never had to use the torch to stave off attackers. Many years later when he was attacked one night he was minus his faithful companion, the torch. The torch, after years of useful service had given up the ghost and Khokababu had not been able to find a similar one to replace it.

The large, joint Bose family had to conform to Khokababu's exacting hours dictated by cinema show timings. Breakfast was at 11 a.m., lunch at 3 p.m. Tea at 8 p.m and dinner at 1 a.m.

Friends and relatives would think twice and shudder to invite the Boses for a meal. They always held up every party by arriving late, a harrowing hungry wait for hostess and guests. Delicious hot food turning into icicles. My father aptly named them the "Ghosts of the night."

Khokababu followed a Spartan life style. He did not crave for any luxuries; he did not have any addictions. He was well satisfied with the basic necessities but he only had two weaknesses. A cup of perfectly brewed Makaibari tea and *rosogollas.* Unfortunately, nobody in his large household could produce the perfect cup of tea he so desired.

Being a finicky perfectionist with rigid habits, he resorted to his own devices to make tea for himself every morning. His morning started at 11 a.m., an hour when ma and I often visited the Boses and found Khokababu engaged in the ritual of making tea.

The whole exercise of making tea was no less intricate than a Japanese tea ceremony. I would watch fascinated as the little man flitted around, following a set pattern of arranging every item required, for this ritual, in their proper places with rapt attention.

He would measure the exact amount of water required, pour it into the little kettle and set it to boil on the kerosene stove in the corner. He would watch the kettle like a hawk until the water reached the exact temperature. He would pour a little of the boiling water in the glazed, heavy brown clay English tea pot which he claimed was the only type fit for making tea. He would swirl the hot water in the tea pot, pour it into the large, bone china, breakfast tea cup and cover it with the saucer to keep warm.

The air tight bottle containing the finest aromatic champagne tea leaves of Makaibari would be opened, the exact amount measured on a silver tea spoon and dropped into the dark hot bowels of the tea pot. Hot water would follow and stop when the exact level was reached. No more no less.

As he fitted the thick, felt Kashmiri embroidered tea cozy on the tea pot, he would note the time on the wall clock. Now he would set about warming the milk, empty the tea cup. Exactly at the dot of 5 minutes, he would whip off the tea cozy, open the tea pot lid, give the liquid a good stir with the same silver tea spoon and pour out the steaming golden liquid into the tea cup.

The whole room filled with the heady aroma of freshly brewed tea. A few drops of milk percolated through a silver strainer and turned the clear liquid murky. Two tea spoons of sugar followed, a quick stir and his tea was ready at last. His little hands flitted about swiftly as each item used was put back in its proper place.

Gently he would put the cup on the table in front of him, shut his eyes and deeply breathe in the exotic aroma that rose to his nostrils on wisps of curling smoke. He would open his eyes, look at the cup lovingly, longingly, grip the delicate handle with his thumb and three fingers while the little one stuck out at right angles, in a perfect aristocratic genteel fashion and bring it to his lips tenderly, reverently as if he was about to partake of the nectar prepared by the gods.

With the very first sip his eyes would close, his head rested on the back of the chair and a deep sigh of, 'Ah,' would emanate from his lips of total delight and satisfaction. This is the moment he enjoyed and lived for. Savouring each sip, his taut slim body would relax, his face a picture of contentment, peace and joy.

When I was old enough to enjoy tea I would beg him for a cup. I soon realized that he made the best cup of tea in the world with loving care.

His second weakness was *rossogollas.* He could wallop two dozen large *rossogollas* in one sitting without batting an eyelid. This never made any change to his slim figure. Blessed was he without diabetes or cholesterol but then all men die of something. So did he after a short illness not related to his excesses. After he was laid to rest the usual rituals followed. At his *sradh* tons of *rossogollas* were made and distributed to satisfy his soul on its upward journey. The invitees ate *rossogollas,* galore but none could beat his record of two dozen at one go.

By now his large family had dwindled down to his ageing wife and daughter, Gutlu. With father gone Gutlu found it extremely difficult to cope with all the responsibilities of running the cinema hall, looking after the house and keeping her job. Every night she came back home mentally and physically exhausted.

Alone in her bedroom she cried for help and strength. Help came in the form of a light caress on her arm, a pat on the head, a fleeting shadow. The sagging of the mattress beside her as if somebody was sitting next to her to keep her company. She felt the constant presence of an invisible being trying to console and lift up her spirits.

The dog would suddenly raise her head and follow something with her eyes around the room wagging her tail or whimpering. A pat on the head by an invisible hand quietened her. The uncanny presence of someone in her room all the time, ceased to bother her, in fact her loneliness disappeared but worries remained.

She had neither faith in God or man but sheer desperation drove her to a man known as the *Mata* for advice, and consolation. She went at the advice of a friend who had great faith in this holy man who could foresee the past, present and future and steer the faithful from disaster and impending danger.

Even the most diehard skeptic clutch at straws before going under. So she found herself at the little temple full of goddesses and the *mata* praying at their feet in a track suit and baseball hat. Her instincts told her to flee from this imposter but better sense prevailed and she sat down.

The *mata* a stocky, unassuming, simple little man was disarmingly frank and charming. She reluctantly voiced her worries and woes. He prescribed *poojas* and certain gem stones to be worn. Gutlu was disappointed and unimpressed.

Then he looked at her face intently and said, "Your father is with you constantly at home." at this she laughed outright and told him that he had died four years ago. "Yes, I know but it is his spirit that lives in the house to help you and console you. He was a short, slim, fair man with glasses, always in a *dhuti.*" he said with his eyes closed as if he could see him clearly in his mind's eye. This apt description of her father did not surprise her. He was a very well known figure in Kalimpong. Everybody knew him by sight, the *mata* must have seen him too.

"His is a good spirit but all spirits need rest," he continued. "What must I do to give his soul rest?" she asked suddenly aware that the invisible presence in her room was none other than her father's spirit. "Do a *puja* at home for the repose of his soul and offer him all the things he loved to eat, like *rossogollas.*" This man is not saying anything positive, she thought, suppressing a smile. Every fool knows that Bengalis love *rossogollas,* "Offer him tea. He loved tea didn't he?" continued the man smiling.

At this Gutlu started and stared at him in disbelief. How could he know Khokababu's weakness for tea, only the immediate family members were aware of it? "Yes, I will follow your instructions," she whispered reverently, a flicker of faith, hope and admiration for this man in a track suit and baseball hat, dawned on her at last.

On an auspicious day as Gutlu was preparing for the *puja,* for the repose of Khokababu's soul, her best friend, Devika, arrived flustered and agitated with a brand new, neatly rolled, black umbrella exactly like the one he used. "I had a vivid dream last night," she said. "Your father appeared to me large as life and asked me for an umbrella. Here it is."

The umbrella, *rossogollas* and Makaibari tea, in his favourite cup, were offered reverently in front of his garlanded photo for the repose of his gentle, considerate soul.

These offering must have fulfilled and satisfied Khokababu's earthly desires and longings once and for all because, he never came back to keep Gutlu company any more.

Terror in the Night

It was summer time, during the day it was hot, nights much cooler. I was busy preparing for my half yearly examination. At the end of the year I would have to face the Senior Cambridge examination so better to get ready from now.

I persuaded ma to let me sleep in the large guest room so that I could study till late at night without disturbing her. The main purpose was not to be involved in learning dull subjects but to read story books!

I was a book worm and poured over story books at every opportunity I got. Now such opportunities were getting less and less as ma kept a strict watch on me, to see that I stuck to my text books rather than my story books. Under the circumstances, if I got the guest room all to myself, it would be the ideal solution. Ma reluctantly agreed. I was overjoyed. I remember reading 'Dracula' one night and finishing it at four o'clock in the morning without ma's knowledge.

The guest room was large and airy with a magnificent view of the Kanchanjungha through the wide bay window. On either side of the bay window, were two small windows which I kept open, for the cool night air to flow in freely. To my dismay, on windy nights, the flowing air played a boisterous, merry game with the curtains. The curtains were flung around with gay abandon. They flapped loudly and rode gleefully from side to side on the smooth curtain rails, making the most unholy racket and disturbing my sleep.

Tired of being disturbed by the frolicking wind and wayward curtains, I decided to put an end to their nightly capers. I bunched up the curtains at either end of the bay window, tied them firmly with a string, strangling them for good measure.

This proved to be a very stupid and hazardous move on my part which manifested itself very soon. Once the curtains were drawn back at night, all my movements in my well lit room were clearly visible from outside. Although the guest room was on the first floor, people passing through Monjula, at night, could easily keep track of my nightly routine and movements through the bay window.

I was not worried about any intruders, as *chors* were rare in Kalimpong and we did not possess anything of great value to attract them. Moreover, ma and I were not absolutely alone, we had company. A young man and a sturdy French Buddhist nun staying in our annexe. Our *kanchi,* lived in too. The presence of three extra people in Monjula made me feel secure and complacent. I felt it was perfectly safe to keep the two small windows open and the curtains drawn at night. Well, I was wrong.

The young man happened to be my Hindi teacher from St. Joseph's Convent. A country bumpkin from Bihar. His qualifications were of no importance to the nuns who gladly appointed him, simply because he could read and write Hindi. Hindi teachers were hard to come by so they grabbed him with delight without paying the slightest attention to his capabilities as a teacher. He fitted their conservative bill perfectly.

A thin, tall, dark, shy much married man with two small children. His family was conveniently left behind, in some obscure village, while he had come to seek his fortune in Kalimpong. Not only was he like a fish out of water in this strange place but specially in St. Joseph's Convent amongst a gaggle of giggling, snickering girls.

He could neither teach nor contain us. His classes were free for all. We continuously badgered him and pulled his leg. He was the butt of all our jokes. The teacher from the next classroom had to appear regularly to maintain order in ours.

He never dared to go and complain to Mother Superior about us as she couldn't understand any Hindi and he couldn't speak any English. He suffered in silence at our hands. We never found out his name, we addressed him simply as *Masterji.* He was eventually replaced by Mrs. Chettri who was also an easy prey to our antics.

Anila, the other inhabitant of Monjula, was a Buddhist nun always dressed in a *bokhu.* It was rumoured that she was a spy. She lived in Kalimpong but disappeared for months trekking and mountain climbing in Sikkim. She therefore owned some climbing gear. The handiest being her ice pick. This always stood near her door to be used as a weapon if necessary. She was mighty strong and if she ever used it, it would be with devastating effect.

The third person present was our newly acquired *kanchi.* A sour faced, middle-aged woman, who professed to be absolutely alone in this world. With no friend or family to visit, she never went out of Monjula.

That fateful night, *kanchi* was not in Monjula. She had suddenly remembered a long forgotten aunt who needed to be visited urgently. She asked ma for two days leave. Ma gladly obliged as she had never taken leave till then.

With *Kanchi* gone, ma and I had early dinner, locked up the house securely and retired to bed. As usual, I drew back the offending curtains of the bay window and opened the two small windows at the two ends. I switched on the table lamp, settled down cozily in the king size bed, entombed by the mosquito net to read.

Soon after, I switched off the light and fell asleep.

Suddenly I was aware of a metallic sound at one of the windows. I was too tired and sleepy to investigate the cause. I just turned over, covered my ear with the blanket to block out the annoying noise and dozed off again. The sound persisted so I decided to put an end to it once and for all. I turned once more and faced the offending window.

I heard a whisper. Surely ma couldn't be whispering to somebody down below, standing at my window in the middle of the night? With a start I realised that both my bedroom doors were locked and bolted.

There was no way ma could enter my room. Who was whispering then?

I peered into the darkness, trying to catch the whispers. The hook of the window was still rattling but why, there was no wind. As my eyes grew accustomed to the darkness, the silhouette of the head and shoulder, of a man, appeared framed at the open window.

There was no doubt now, that it was an intruder sitting on my window hook about to enter my room. Suddenly goose bumps appeared on my arms and legs. Stark terror gripped me. My whole body was numb with fear but it was this very fear that switched on my numb brain into action.

I realised that if the *chor*, obviously he was a *chor*, who invades a house in the middle of the night but a *chor*, jumped into my room and I showed signs of waking, he would surely harm me. Even kill me but if I raised an alarm right now, he would jump down from the window and disappear. He would certainly not rush in, to be apprehended.

With this simple calculation in mind I tried to scream. However much I tried, no sound would come out of my vocal cords, constricted with fear and my parched mouth. The thief would step in any minute. The more desperate I got the tighter my throat muscles became and refused to let out any sound at all.

I made one last desperate effort. A deep, hoarse sound burst out of my dry throat. A sound so gruesome that I didn't recognize it as my own. More like the bray of an injured donkey in throes of great pain. It was not a loud sound but a sound that was the consorted effort of my whole petrified body. It had taken all my courage and strength to produce that single inhuman sound. It did the trick.

The figure at the window clearly disappointed by his aborted mission just mouthed two words disgusted, "She is up." I heard him jump down on to the wide ledge below the window and down to the ground. Next I heard many footsteps galloping down the drive, as loudly as a pack of wild horses. So, there was not just one *chor* but a whole gang.

Sheer relief coursed through my numb terror stricken body, soaked in perspiration. I could move my arms and legs once more and my long lost gagged voice surfaced again. I started screaming at the top of my voice. I called out to ma, then added all the names of the people present or absent in Monjula. I screamed for Bahadur, the *mali*, two male members who never stayed overnight in Monjula. The string of names was meant to warn the *chors* that Monjula was teeming with people, in case; they had intentions of making a second foray.

My frantic, terrified screams woke ma up. She came to my locked door, half asleep, grumbling, "How many times have I told you not to read ghost stories at bed time. This is the result. You are having terrible nightmares. Serves you right. Now open the door."

Now that danger was over and ma was at hand, I found I was stuck to the bed. The very thought of getting out of bed, crossing the floor in the dark or open the door for her was too much of an effort. My limbs once stiff, now turned to jelly refusing to obey my commands. "Open the door," ma shouted. With great difficulty I managed to extricate myself from my wet, sweat sodden bed, lifted the unwieldy mosquito curtain and stumbled to the door. It never occurred to me to switch on the table lamp next to my bed.

Ma rushed in, switched on the lamp, angry at this rude interruption of her sleep. "Don't you ever read those frightening stories at night again!"

"But ma, I didn't have a nightmare, there was a thief at my window," I breathed white-faced and shaken.

"There see, you did have a nightmare," she exclaimed smugly.

"No, no, it was not a nightmare; a man was sitting on my window sill about to get in when I screamed. He exclaimed, 'She is up,' jumped down and ran away with his gang. Didn't you hear them running?"

Suddenly the truth sunk in. Ma sat down heavily on my bed and held me tight. Her whole body trembled with fear. I clung to her. After a long time she controlled herself and ran to the back verandah overlooking the annexe and started screaming, "*Chor, chor*!"

Anila heard her frantic cries and came out instantly to find out what the matter was. Once informed about the *chor*, she came running out with her combat weapon, the ice pick, torch and scoured the grounds for the offending intruder. Ma called frantically to the only man in this house, *Masterji* but no answer. He did not appear on the scene till dawn.

Ma and I were sitting huddled up unable to sleep when we heard *Masterji's* faint voice, "*Chor hai ki nahi hai?*" Ma lost all her composure and ran out to confront him. "What kind of a man are you?" she yelled. "You are the only man in the house and you didn't come out when you heard my cries for help. You hid in your room, now you peep out of the window and ask if the *chor* is here or not? You are a coward, a despicable caricature of a man. Anila, a woman, came to our help but you did not come out!"

Ma's outburst had no effect on him, he was neither humiliated nor shamed, he started to give an explanation in his casual lazy drawl. "Mrs. Mitter, you know I am a married man with two small children, how could I take the risk of facing a dangerous *chor*? What if I got killed in the encounter, who would look after my wife and children?"

From that day we referred to him as "*Chor hai ki, nahi hai. Masterji.*"

Kanchi was back the next day looking innocent but we were convinced that she was the inside informer and disappeared to save her skin in case the operation went sour.

For years, I couldn't sleep in a room alone. Long after I was married, I would wake my husband, at all hours of the night, if I heard the slightest sound, to check if there was a *chor* around. I used to see the silhouette of a head and shoulders even in my sleep. This traumatic experience of my early teens left a deep, indelible scar which dulled over the years but still haunts me.

The Super Star

One summer, somebody rented the cottage just above our house called Panoroma II. Although the cottage was close enough, we were not able to see the inhabitants on account of the row of cherry trees dividing the two houses.

Ma, incorrigibly sociable, never wasted any time making friends with all new comers. She went out of her way to help them, advise them and feed them until they happily settled down in Kalimpong. This time I noticed, to my great surprise, that ma was not making any move to visit the new comer next door. No sounds emanated from that house, especially not of exuberant children so I lost all interest in it. Ma showed no interest either.

A few days later, I overheard this conversation between ma and Somda, a young man, which gave me the clue to ma's stoical indifference to the new comer next door. Somda was brimming with excitement as he asked ma, "*Didi,* have you met Kananbala as yet?" "No." "Why not? She is staying next door to you and you haven't visited her yet?" he asked incredulously. "*Didi,* what a marvelous opportunity to meet the Super Star, the darling of the silver screen, a great celebrity right at your door step and you haven't made any effort to meet her?"

"No, Som, I haven't met her and I don't intend to. She has not stepped out of that house since she has arrived. May be, she is here incognito, looking for some peace and quiet, away from the prying eyes of fans like you and reporters. I have no wish to invade her privacy, in fact nobody should."

"In-cognito indeed, everybody in Kalimpong town knows she is here. Can anybody famous as she, cover her tracks? The public adore her. In town the Bengalis are planning a huge reception for her. In fact, I have come to invite her. Since I have never met her, I thought I could ask you to introduce me to her. I was sure you had met her several times by now and become best of friends." "I have no desire to make friends with an actress." ma finished.

"But *Didi*, she is no cheap, run of the mill actress. She is a Super Star, not only of Bengal but whole of India. What an opportunity you are missing. People line up in the streets to get a glimpse of her. They queue up for hours to buy a ticket for her shows. Her movies run for months. Her fans would give their right arms to get to know her and you are not making any move to see her! really *Didi*, you are impossible."

"Yes, Yes, I know how famous she is, what a wonderful actress she is. I have enjoyed her performances both on the stage and screen. I admire her art but that is no reason why I should fall on my knees and adore her like the rest of her fans. I do know all about her, I do not wish to hob-nob with famous actresses, in my opinion they are all infamous. I do not want to have anything to do with her. You go and invite her yourself. Don't invite me to the reception, that is final."

Ma, a mighty moralist with a purinitical attitude to boot, having been weaned on Sarat Chandra's novels which decried wine, women and song, kept her distance from shady characters. Ma had heard unmitigated rumors of actress's life styles and exploits on and off the stage. According to her a decent woman never displayed herself so provocatively on the stage for the whole world to see. They were all shameless women with no vestige of morality or decency who joined this degrading profession. They led a sinful life, glorified *Nautch* girls.

Days passed Kalimpong's people had lost interest in Kanan Devi because she refused to meet anyone. One morning I saw her *mali,* come down to our house screaming, "Memsahib, memsahib, please come quickly, the ayah has cracked her skull, please come, she is bleeding profusely," he finished breathlessly. Ma not wasting any time rushed up the narrow path connecting our two houses. I was not going to miss out on this one and the only opportunity to see the Star. I followed ma at a safe distance, knowing she wouldn't allow me to come in contact with the fallen Star.

The *mali,* led her to the dining room. Two women were standing there. One in a white *saree,* was sobbing quietly, holding her forehead with one hand while blood dripped through her fingers. With the other hand she was wiping away her tears. I stood at the door and watched amazed. I had never seen an adult, except ma, shedding tears before. The other petite woman in a mousy grey *saree,* stood wringing her hands helplessly, looking totally bewildered. The bleeding ayah, obviously in great pain, was standing respectfully.

Ma took in the situation at a glance. Ignoring the woman in grey, she gently eased the ayah on a chair. "Quick, get me some Dettol, iodine, cloth and scissors," ma ordered to nobody in particular. The handwringing little woman darted off in a great hurry to the bedroom as if the clapper had sounded, somebody had called 'action' and the cameras started rolling. She soon returned with the necessary items and laid them carefully on the table. Ma went about silently bandaging the injured woman with exaggerated concentration.

This diversion gave me time to look around. I was looking for Kananbala but there was no sign of the beautiful, glamorous Super Star. I was very disappointed.

Operation bandage over, ma asked the injured woman how she had managed to hurt herself. "I was cleaning the fireplace. I stood up suddenly and banged my head on the sharp corner of the mantle piece," she said. Ma patted her on the shoulder and turned to the woman in grey to give instructions of after care of the patient when she spotted me standing, open mouthed, by the door, her face turned into a thunder cloud but she continued speaking. The woman in grey looked relieved; she managed a Monalisa smile as she thanked ma. There was no reciprocating smile on ma's face as she grabbed my hand and marched me out of the house unceremoniously.

All hell broke loose once we reached home. "Who told you to go there?" she asked me sternly. "I wanted to see Kananbala," I blurted out terrified. "Now that you have seen her, are you happy? You are never to go up there again." "I never saw her," I wailed. Ma burst out laughing. "Of course you saw her; she was there large as life." "Where?" "Why, the lady in a grey *saree*." "That was Kananbala?" I breathed incredulously. She was not wearing any jewellery, a gorgeous silk *saree*, most important of all; she was not wearing any make up. She didn't look grand as I had expected an actress to look. She looked as plain as any other woman, not even as beautiful as ma.

Out of the blue Kananbala arrived at our doorstep, Monjula, one afternoon. Ma was frosty but gracious as she invited her in. "I just came to thank you for all the help that you gave me that day," she said shyly.

Ma's conversation and actions of serving tea were of exaggerated politeness. I don't think anybody had ever treated the Star with such cool, gracious and studied indifference. She was used to adulation of people who gushed and swooned all around her not this cold reception. Perhaps, this attitude of ma's made her feel at ease, more like a normal human being.

I stared at her sitting on the opposite chair. She was wearing an ordinary cotton *saree*. Her long black tresses, neatly rolled up in a big *khopu*, lay on the nape of her neck. Her oval face devoid of any make up was quite ordinary except for her large, doe like, expressive eyes that lit up her face. Yes, that was it, the secret of her success, her beautiful eyes.

As ma's frostiness gradually melted, Kananbala visited us daily, taking great precaution to come when there were no guests in Monjula.

She would happily join ma in whatever activity she was involved in, cooking, sewing, knitting or just cutting vegetables. She loved these simple household chores which made ma realise her inherent need to be a plain and simple housewife.

I enjoyed her company too. She would play snakes and ladders, ludo or carrom with me for hours with great gusto.

It was my birthday and as usual lots of people had been invited for a tea party. Kananbala enthusiastically offered to help ma with the cooking. Ma skeptical about her cooking abilities agreed reluctantly. She arrived early in the afternoon and set about making *luchies*.

Ma had planned to give her a much simpler job but she insisted on rolling out *luchies* with great enthusiasm. To ma's surprise and delight she rolled out perfectly round little *luchi* which ballooned up when deep fried. "Where did you learn to make such perfect *lunchies?*" ma asked astonished. "Oh, my mother taught me when I was a little girl," she replied casually but visibly pleased at the compliment. The best actress award couldn't have pleased her more.

She disappeared long before the party started. Baba was just as surprised at her expertise and couldn't stop telling people about it for years, how Kananbala had made perfect little *luchies*, for his daughter's birthday, of course, nobody believed him.

Ma never pried into Kananbala's past and certainly not the present. She was happy to know her as she appeared here and now. A simple, sincere, caring individual like any other but absolutely charming and intelligent. She on her own started relating nostalgic memories of her childhood to ma.

She came from a very respectable, middle class but poor Bengali family. She had no choice but to join the films at an early age for financial reasons. She was readily accepted since it was difficult to find women, especially from respectable families, to join the films. She had started at the bottom rung and risen to the very pinnacle of her trade through sheer hard work, she maintained.

"Charudi, nobody realises the sweat, tears, hard work and heart break that goes on behind the silver screen. They think we film artists lead a frivolous life of leisure, pleasure and comfort, far from it," she would sigh. She would relate to ma about the hours spent on memorizing her part and gruelling practice sessions.

Mastering her acting skills depicting joy, sorrow, sadness, elation, tears, laughter, the dewy eyed ecstasy of first love and a myriad other expressions with feeling which had to be honed to perfection before she appeared in front of the whirring cameras and glaring flood lights. Scene after scene had to be shot over and over again until perfect. There were no stunt women so she had to learn to swim, ride, drive, sing and dance till her feet almost fell off.

Ma started to realise from Kanan Devi's outpouring, the difficult and lonely lives, the much maligned film stars lead, with no time for a normal life or to raise a family.

Always in the limelight, admired by scores of fans but no sincere friend. A life of heart break, disappointments, tears and sacrifice lay behind the glamorous larger than life images on the Silver Screen. A bird imprisoned in a golden cage.

The day of Kananbala's departure arrived. As she said goodbye to ma, genuine tears of sorrow welled up in her beautiful large eyes. Ma's original disapproval had turned to firm friendship that lasted all their lives. Ma had got to love the simple, sincere, lonely Kananbala and admire the woman of guts and determination who had conquered all odds to become a Super Star.

Hungry Lion!

Every year bands of guests came to spend their summer holidays at Monjula. They came from Calcutta and other parts of India, wherever temperature soared, for a cool restful holiday in Kalimpong.

This time, baba was bringing his friend with him, Kantibabu, who lived in Santiniketan. An elderly gentleman who spent all his time at home translating Omar Khayyam. I had visited his small compact house in Santiniketan where he lived with his Hungarian wife, Eta.

Years ago, Kantibabu, a confirmed bachelor, on his travels through Hungary, had met this buxom young woman, a farmer's daughter, fallen hopelessly in love, married and brought her back to India.

Kantibabu, a short, slight man with thinning hair, rimless spectacles, had delicate features compared to his strapping young wife's florid homely ones. The age difference between them was 20 years.

Once in India Kantibabu set about educating his wife just as the famous Professor Higgins had done with Eliza, in My Fair Lady. Eta knew how to milk cows, plant, sow, reap and rear farm animals but there her expertise ended.

Kantibabu painstakingly taught her to read, write, and speak English and Bengali fluently. Her Bengali was heavily laced with Hungarian accent. Education was necessary so was Bengali etiquette and the intricacies of wrapping six yards of seamless cloth, a *saree*, around Eta's huge figure.

Kantibabu, a quiet, mild, even tempered man, had enormous patience with his high spirited, lively young wife. He managed to cut, polish, domesticate and upgrade her from a rustic hand to a Bengali *Bou.* No mean feat this, no less an achievement than Mr. Higgins.'

Everybody marveled at the transformation. She blended into Santiniketan's Tagore-oriented society quite easily.

One can change a person completely in every respect but to tame one is not always possible. Eta had a mind and ideas of her own which she imposed on everyone. Endowed with robust health, she was vigorous, full of boundless, nervous energy so acute, that she couldn't sit still for a single moment. In those days, such over-excitement and activity was not attributed to hypertension. It was considered quite natural and normal in one's behavior.

Baba arrived with Kantibabu from Siliguri in a taxi. Since they didn't have much luggage, baba decided to get down at Kali *Mandir* gate, walk up Atisha Road and get home. The two walked up the steep slope of Atisha Road, reached my uncle's house, Arunachal and walked in.

It was tea-time and my aunt, an English lady, always produced good, strong tea with an array of mouth watering tea time delicacies. This was too great a temptation and couldn't be missed so the two friends sat down to a sumptuous tea and arrived home in high spirits.

Kantibabu did not display any signs of fatigue after his long journey. He heartily joined all the other guests in the evening for a long session of socializing and eating.

We all had dinner and trooped upstairs to bed but no sign of ma and baba. They were still downstairs with Kantibabu who had been allotted the single bedroom there. Soon, all the adults descended downstairs in a hurry leaving us children to go to sleep.

There were five of us children, our ages ranging from 5 to 14. We realised that something was going on downstairs and it was out of bounds for us. This whetted our curiosity so we stuck out ears to the wooden floor to listen to the activities downstairs. The wooden floor acted as a taut drum and every sound came through clearly to our ears.

I could hear ma's voice, it sounded agitated, "Kantibabu, please sip this warm water and try to relax." Baba's voice was grim and worried. "We should call Dr. Boral but he won't come at this time of the night and there is no way of calling him." We did not have a phone neither did the few houses on Atisha Road. Dr. Boral didn't have a car.

Now Kantibabu's voice, rather faint, came through clearly. "I am feeling weak and uneasy in the stomach." ma's voice, "Try and drink this Aqua Ptychotis. It will soothe your stomach and drive away all the gas." This was ma's panacea for all stomach problems. I knew it well as it seared my mouth every time she made me take it. The others were talking in whispers trying to figure out exactly what was wrong. The one word we kept hearing was "indigestion."

So that was it, indigestion and why not, Kantibabu's stomach attuned to Eta's simple and frugal meals had suddenly been over loaded with tons of rich pastries, cakes, etc at tea and then by a sumptuous dinner soon after. Surely the poor stomach couldn't be blamed for reacting so violently to such excesses, after years of abstinence.

We were sleepy and tired. We lost interest in the man with indigestion downstairs. We went to bed and fell in to the deep untroubled slumber of childhood.

Next morning, we woke up to find all the parents missing. Only Indu *mashi,* keeping guard over us. "Now children you are not to go downstairs. You stay right here, your breakfast will be brought to you." she pronounced in a heavy serious tone. "But why?" we asked mystified. "Never mind, do as you are told." Gablu, the eldest amongst us asked, "Why are we being punished, we haven't done anything wrong?" "No, you haven't, now, just be good and do as you are told."

We were very curious about what was going on downstairs. We crowed around the bay window our noses flattened on the glass pane to look out. People were very quiet, talking in hushed tones. "The old man must be very ill" said Bulu. Dr. Boral arrived. Our nearest neighbours came too.

Then we saw our *mali* and other servants making a bamboo bier on the lawn. We watched in shocked silence. "He is dead!," pronounced Gablu and so he was. Dr. Boral's diagnosis was, a massive heart attack. Kantibabu must have been too frail to take the steep climb up Atisha Road, tuck in an enormous tea and dinner which proved too much for his poor heart and stomach.

We were not allowed to come down until all the rituals for the dead were over and the body taken for cremation. None of us had seen a dead body except for Gablu who had lost his father. Our parents were foolishly trying to protect us from the horrors of death instead of steeling us against the inevitability of it, a fact of life.

Now started a massive hunt for Eta. For some reason, unknown to us, the couple had decided to go on separate holidays this year. She had gone to Kodaikanal, the hill station in the south and he to Kalimpong. Nobody knew where or with whom she was staying. She needed to be informed immediately about her dear husband's sudden demise.

Ma started looking through Kantibabu's papers frantically. No address of Eta's could be found. She found a couple of letters written by Eta to Kantibabu from Kodaikanal minus address or dates.

Ma was furious "All these highly educated people of this world, degree holders, consider themselves educated, when they don't even know how to write a letter. It is something one learns at school. Address of the writer and date comes first. But they don't write it. They don't know. Educated indeed! Now, how am I ever going to find her?" she cried throwing up her arms in despair.

Ma was not a degree holder but prided herself on the fact that she was far more knowledgeable than any highly qualified degree holder. She could hold her own in any serious discussion, could read, write and speak English fluently and of course, write articles, stories and letters correctly.

Baba vaguely remembered Kantibabu mentioning that Eta was visiting a Bengali family called Chackerburty in Kodaikanal. "There can't be more than one Bengali family in Kodaikanal, so let me send them a telegram" said baba. There was no other means of communication available and no other option. The telegram was a complete shot in the dark but it worked.

One afternoon we saw Eta striding up the drive in a great hurry. After the initial burst of sorrow and a few days of mourning for her dead husband, she settled down very well in Monjula to spend the rest of her holiday in Kalimpong.

In her voluminous *saree,* with her brown hair in a small *khopa,* she was an Amazon. The short, stout Bengali ladies and men were puny compared to her. She looked exactly like *Chachi* no. 420 – the part of the *chachi,* enacted by Kamal Hassan in the movie of that name.

As her sorrow wore off, her nervous energy took over. She couldn't stay still for a moment. She was everywhere, driving the easy going, slow, languid, laid back Bengali population of our house to distraction.

Ma couldn't perform any household duties without Eta rushing to help her and take over the job in hand only to ruin it. She took over the servant's job at the dining table. Like a charging bull she barged into everyone's way, thereby irritating them no end. Ma refused to hear any complaints about her from anybody. "Don't you see she has just lost her husband, she needs to keep herself occupied to forget her sorrow? After all, she is only trying to help." So the meddling busybody was given a free hand to merrily carry on with her own irksome devices.

We children sat at a separate table and the adults close by. Baba kept his guests well entertained, at table, with stories and jokes. This meant, he took longer to finish the food on his plate. Eta managed to tuck in an enormous quantity of food in record time. She was always the first to finish then, she would shoot out of her chair and start collecting the empty plates from the table. Baba disliked this habit as she distracted the diners by jumping up like a jack in the box and his jokes went unheard.

The last straw was, when having dinner one night; baba lifted his fork and spoon to put a morsel of food in his mouth. When he lowered his cutlery, they fell with a bang on the table because his plate had been whipped off. Although livid with Eta at that moment, he considered it a huge joke and later repeated it to his guests, to amuse them.

We children were not spared. She was always lecturing us about good manners, behaviour, does and don'ts. We were fed up with her and gave her a wide berth. We had to find a pseudo name for her so no one would know when we were referring to her. I found the perfect one 'Hungry Lion' in keeping with her huge appetite.

Every night, our dessert was delicious sweet mango pulp with thick creamy *Kheer*. Ma made the pulp by squeezing each *langra* into a bowl. Eta wanted to help and took this duty upon herself. Just by chance, I happened to see Eta at this chore. She was doing a better job of squeezing each *langra* dry with her powerful hands. In the process, some pulp slid down her long arms. To my disgust, she licked the flowing pulp all the way up from elbow to hands, licked her fingers clean with great relish, dripping saliva and then, started on the next one!

I told the children the way the mango pulp was being made *jutha*, every night by Eta. That night, ma was surprised when all the children refused to eat their favourite dessert. I quietly told ma the reason and she very diplomatically managed to relieve Eta off that task.

Summer rains and my dysentery started at the same time. It started with gripes in my stomach. "Indigestion," proclaimed ma sending me into a panic. It was a condition I dreaded ever since Kantibabu had so suddenly died of it, although, Dr. Boral had diagnosed heart attack. I was sure I would die of it sometime in the night. Death was scary now that I had witnessed it at close quarters.

I was glad to be alive next day but my condition worsened. High temperature and frequent motions left me limp and exhausted. The only reason ma deduced for my dysentery, were the hard green peaches in the garden. "You have been at those peaches?" she asked me. "Yes, but all the others had them too." I replied, defiantly. "But you have a very weak constitution they don't." That was true.

I was a pampered, protected and a sickly child without any immunity and caught every single disease doing the round in Kalimpong, in its severest form. My green dysentery turned to blood dysentery, Dr. Boral was called. He arrived in pouring rain and dispensed an array of pills, potions and the famous liquid, carminative mixture. His medicines had no effect on me.

My dysentery was out of his control. Extremely worried, he asked ma's permission to bring in Dr. (Miss) Macllen, the chief medical officer from Charteris Hospital. The only hospital in Kalimpong. A tall, pleasant Scottish lady, she looked grim after examining me. She prescribed more pills and left.

I could see the tension and worry writ large on ma and baba's faces. The guests were subdued, the children spoke in whispers and padded around the house quietly. Now I was sure I was going to give up the ghost and clung to ma. I recovered slowly.

The rains persisted, bringing in its wake the worst disaster in the annals of Kalimpong's and Darjeeling's history till them. The disaster of 1950. Massive landslides came crashing down, blocking all roads, felling trees, telegraph and electric lines. Water pipes, buried three fee under ground, lay exposed and broken. The situation in Monjula was chaotic with no water, electricity, coal, food, a sick child and a house full of guests.

Ma and baba were in a tizzy but now, Eta's super energy came to the fore. Hitching up her *saree,* girding her *anchal,* tightly, she set to work. She collected buckets of rain water for the choked toilets, fire wood from the garden, walked over precarious landsides to the market to bring medicines for me and look for food in the nearby villages. She took full control of the helpless, lackadaisical, laid back guests, organizing them into groups to go to the swollen *jhora* nearby, to wash their clothes and take baths. She activated and motivated them to be useful, helpful rather than being dependent on ma who was exhausted. She was whizzing like a dynamo, around the house, getting things done very efficiently.

Feeling a bit better, I was sitting at the bay window upstairs when I noticed a procession tramping purposefully up the drive, well clad in raincoats and gumboots with big umbrellas. It was headed by Mr. R.N Dutta, our neighbour, a big man followed by his little English wife and two daughters, Roma and Betty. They reached the verandah downstairs where ma and baba were sitting. Mr. Dutt announced that he and his family had come to stay in Monjula as the hill side behind their cottage had come sliding down. Tons of mud and water had gushed into the house forcing them out.

He had neither sent an S.O.S nor asked for permission to invade Monjula. He lived close enough to do so. He took it for granted that the Mitters would be honoured to have him and his family as their guest. Already Monjula was bursting at the seams with guests. Their arrival put a tremendous strain on the dwindling resources of Monjula.

The children were not allowed to come into my room in case of infection, so I lay in bed sadly listening to their laughter and pattering feet. They were oblivious of the calamity that had befallen Kalimpong and Monjula.

Mrs. Dutt, an angel of an English lady, came to sit by me, talk to me and read me stories. She was the only one who realised how lonely and dejected I felt. Her daughter Betty compassionate like her mother, wide eyed and timid, would come to visit me surreptitiously.

Illness meant starvation which turned out to be worse than the disease. I was better now but kept on a frugal unappetizing diet of barley water and gooey rice. My empty stomach screamed for solid food. My mouth filled with saliva every time I thought of chicken roast, mutton curry, even plain *dal* and rice. I was desperate for food.

I managed to convince the innocent Betty that she should smuggle up some food for me every day or I would die. Betty, whenever she could, would squirrel away tit bits for my survival. A bun, a boiled egg, a delicious meringue, a bowl of vegetable curry. Oh! How delicious these morsels of forbidden food tasted. I will never forget.

The disaster proved to be just wonderful for us children without a care in the world. Once pronounced fit and able, I joined the band of children once more. We ran up and down every squelching mud slide. Went to the cascading *jhora* for baths. The crystal clear water bounded over rocks and boulders breaking its momentum into sprays.

I was glad to be alive and enjoying every moment of this unexpected freedom. No school for me as all schools had shut down, enough friends, no routine, no restrictions. We were having the time of our lives. We were surprised when our leader and mentor Gablu suddenly lost all interest in our childish activities. The reason was soon clear, he had fallen madly in love with the vivacious, pretty, young lady who had arrived in our midst, Roma. Gablu mooned, swooned and followed her around like a love sick puppy. We, tired of his stupidity, excluded him from all our games.

Soon the road to Siliguri opened, all the guests departed in a hurry. Monjula was empty once more. Eta went back to Santaniketan and eventually to Hungary where she died

Gablu went back to Kolkata but his sickness did not leave him. Every week, he sent a message to his "Fairy Princess," through the personal column of The Statesman for months. Roma was tickled pink by this gesture but made no move to encourage or soothe his bleeding heart.

Gablu, a grandfather now, becomes starry-eyed and nostalgic whenever his Fairy Princess is mentioned. It is not because she occupies a place in his heart but she brings back sweet memories of the awakening of first love.

Visitors of Yore

Apart from the gentleman who arrived in Kalimpong in the 50s few ladies arrived as well. Two most interesting individuals whom I came in contact with were Miss Carplex, a middle aged lady form Paris and an elderly British lady, Miss Barclay from France. Brits are never without their cats, so she too had her cat Tola in tow.

Miss Carplex took up residence next door to us in Chitrabhanu, Mrs. Pratima Tagore's small flat. Miss Barclay occupied the ground floor of our outhouse in Monjula.ll the foreigners who arrived in Kalimpong, in those days, came with one specific purpose, to learn Tibetan. Miss Carplex was not a student of the Tibetan language. What her business was nobody could fathom, even Miss Barclay had a Tibetan tutor attached to her.

Every morning the Tibetan teacher came to give Miss Barclay lessons. We could hear her thick voice mouthing tongue twisting Tibetan words which didn't sound anywhere near the teacher's pronunciation. He was a proficient teacher and was teaching a number of foreigners but Miss Barclay was beyond his teaching skills. He gave up teaching her in desperation although the fees she paid were more than adequate. Not daunted, Miss Barclay tried out all the other tutors available. They all left her after a few aborted lessons.

To compensate for her inadequate knowledge of the Tibetan language, she became a Tibetan in all other aspects. She donned a *Bokhu* and gave her cook instructions to cook only Tibetan food for her. The *Bokhu,* was a welcome change.

It covered all those protruding tires and fat lumps of her stumpy legs, giving her a dignified look. But there was no way to cover her large fleshy face with drooping jaws and myopic watery eyes.

Miss Carplex on the other hand, was a slim, well proportioned, much younger, attractive lady with a burnished tan she had acquired from generous doses of ultra violet rays of the Kalimpong sun. She wore smart Parisian dresses, short enough to show off her shapely legs. All her efforts to look elegant and pretty were completely detracted by the bandana she always wore. It covered a round smooth head with no hint of hair under it I guessed.

She was pleasant and amiable, while Miss Barclay was not. Miss Barclay barked. Ma ever generous, helpful and friendly would knock at her door to find out if she required anything from the market or just give her company. Sometimes she would usher ma in with open arms or rudely turn her away with "I don't have time for you now." Ma tired of her unpredictable behaviour learnt to keep her distance. This rudeness towards ma infuriated me, a hot tempered school girl. I started ignoring her, also landing a mighty kick on her beloved cat which often sneaked in and made herself comfortable on our divan.

One day Miss Barclay was very rude to ma again. Ma swore never to go near her. Next morning Miss Barclay appeared with a cake. A peace offering, no apology. Ma was well satisfied that Miss Bark, as I called her, had realized her bad behaviour and came to appease her. The cake I never ate. How could she insult ma then expect to be forgiven by a mere cake?

I contacted every childhood disease and was in bed more often than not. Antibiotics were not invented. So I was house bound for days. As soon as I was a little better, I would sit at the window longing to go out and play. Boredom enveloped me. Looking out of our window, one afternoon I spotted Miss Bark labouring up the steps from her house to ours, carrying a small box. She saw me at the window and said, "I have come to play a game of lexicon with you. Please let me in." I was taken aback but very quickly all the insults heaped on ma, by her, surfaced and I said coldly, "I don't have time for you just now," just like the way she used to tell ma and disappeared out of sight.

At that point of time I felt elated, happy that I had paid back the old bag in her own coin. She deserved to be told off. A few days later it dawned on me that she was not as selfish, rude and self centered as everybody branded her. She had spared a thought for me. A youngster suffering more from utter boredom than the disease. She had not come to visit a patient with goodies and shower sympathy but had come with the sole purpose of chasing my boredom away. An act of kindness which I had spurned so thoughtlessly. I felt humbled and thoroughly ashamed of myself.

I did not mention this incident to ma, knowing full well, what her reaction would be. I would have to suffer a lecture from her on good manners, then go and apologize to Miss Bark, only to be turned away rudely by her.

Mr. And Mrs. North came to stay in Chitrabhanu each summer to avoid the scorching heat of Shantiniketan. One year, they brought a young Bengali servant, Dhiren, with them. The young lad was thrilled to find himself amongst so many foreigners. He wanted to adopt their life style but there was no scope for this as he had to conform to his status, in the realms of the servant's world that he lived in.

Frequent parties were held in Monjula and Chitrabhanu. Dhiren was fascinated by them, specially the birthday parties. He found this a novel idea for collecting gifts. He decided he was going to give a birthday party too, not for his colleagues but for the *memsahibs* who would shower him with gifts and money.

He broached this subject to ma and asked for her help. He did not know his date of birth or how old he was. So ma fixed a suitable date. Ma was not quite sure whether the foreigners would accept a servant's invitation or not. The foreigners do not have any class distinction, so they were tickled pink to get his invitation and accepted it.

The birthday lunch was to be held in Mrs. Tagore's dining hall. Since Dhiren would be serving his guests and it would not be proper for him to sit at the table with them, he asked Miss Carplex to preside.

She came dressed to kill for the occasion. We were stunned to see the change in her appearance as she sat regally at the head of the table. She was wearing a long shimmering silk sheath of gold that reached down to her matching stiletto-heeled sandals. Her fingers displayed several gold rings, long painted nails and an enormous solitaire. Her make-up impeccable. The crowning glory was her golden hair, a thick braid of which circled her head. I whispered to ma, "She has such lovely hair, why does she always hide it under a Bandana?" "It is a wig," ma whispered crossly and told me to shut up. She did Dhiren proud to appear in all her finery just as she would have at a Paris ball.

Miss Bark arrived in her shapeless *bokhu* and for once, joined in the spirit of the party, displaying a sense of humour that no one had detected before. We got glimpses of her wit and charm which she kept securely locked up inside her.

Dhiren had worked hard and produced a sumptuous Bengali lunch which everyone enjoyed. Mrs. North felt sorry for him as he couldn't join us at table. He did cut the cake and blew the out the candles as we sang Happy Birthday his eyes filled with tears. He will never experience such a birthday party ever again. I think he will always treasure the memories of this grand birthday party rather than the gifts he craved for and got.

I also remember Dr. Libenthal, a visiting professor at Santiniketan, from Germany who used to come with his wife to Chitrabhanu during summer. The elderly couple was quiet and gentle and devoted to each other. They became firm friends of ma and visited us every evening for tea. Ma was especially fond of Mrs. Libenthal, a kind, demure, sincere, simple house *frau.*

Ma was always happy to see them whenever they came to Kalimpong, until one summer, when the dear old man turned up with a young woman on his wrinkled arm, instead of his devoted wife for tea. He introduced her as Laura, his student, whom he had brought along to look after him as his dear wife had gone to Germany to see her brother. He was not the serious old Professor we knew but a changed man in high spirits.

He expected ma to greet this young woman with open arms and accord her the same friendly treatment that she always meted out to his wife. Ma was furious and maintained a stony silence all through tea, to show her disapproval. The doctor was so hyped with his new found young love that he chatted on with great exuberance, failing to notice ma's dislike of his affair with the young lady.

As soon as they left, ma burst our vehemently, "Just see, that doddering old fool, leaving his wonderful, devoted wife for his young filly. How disgusting. Men are all alike young or old. I don't want to see his face ever again. The old fool doesn't realise that the young woman will empty his pocket and dump him. With what face will he go back to his wonderful wife? Well, if I were her, I would never take the cheating fool back!"

The doctor was too engrossed with his young love to spare time for tea at Monjula. Just as well, it would only infuriate ma further. From our house, which is at a higher level than Chitrabhanu, we would see them frolicking around the garden in true Bollywood fashion!

They left soon and many years later, we heard from common friends about the Libenthals. Ma's predictions had come true. The young female had left the old man high and dry after squandering all his money on clothes and jewellery which he could hardly afford. He had been forgiven and accepted back by his loving wife.

One day Miss Carplex suddenly disappeared without saying goodbye to any of her friends in Kalimpong. What had made her fly off so suddenly and secretively was a mystery. We missed her cherry disposition and were stuck with gloomy old Miss Bark. She had no plans of leaving Kalimpong. She carried on doggedly with her translation of a dictionary from Tibetan to French. Her knowledge of Tibetan was suspect and how many people would require such a dictionary was a million dollar question. This project kept her happy and occupied, sparing people the burden of her boring and irritable company.

Ma and I left for warmer climes of Calcutta as soon as my winter school holidays started. Miss Bark stayed on. Early, one morning, our *chowkidar* spotted an enormous white bundle on the stone slab covering the back drain. He went to investigate and to his horror, found Miss Bark, in her white nightgown, lying in a heap face down. He, with much difficulty, managed to turn her over only to hear a long whistling breath going out of her open mouth. She was stone dead.

The police came to investigate and found no foul play. She had died of a massive heart attack on her way to the toilet.

They also found her unfinished manuscript. The last word she had translated was Farewell.

Football Fellows

In those days Kalimpong was sparsely populated. The summer houses on Atisha Road were few and far between. Their owners appeared briefly during summer. Mr. And Mrs. Chatterjee, ma and I were the only permanent residents. The Chatterjees, a childless elderly couple lived just below us at Parbati, now Pine View. I was the only child on Atisha Road. Only child is always a lonely child, I had no one to play with.

Until I joined school I was quite content in Bahadur's company but having discovered how delightful it was to play with children of my age group, I longed for such company at home. I constantly badgered ma to find company for me. In desperation, she turned to the little village behind our house. She knew all the villagers since they used our private road as a short cut to Atisha Road and also collected their daily supply of drinking water from our garden tap. They had umpteen children, a child bank.

Ma would call out towards the little thatched huts across the gurgling *jhora,* on the hill side, "Oh Thuli *ko amma,* please send Thuli and her sisters to come and play with Monila." Ma's thin voice hardly audible above the bouncing, clamouring waters of the *jhora.* If Thuli's *amma,* happened to be out in her vegetable patch she would hear ma's repeated requests or her voice would just mingle with the waters and flow down the hill.

Thuli's *amma* just couldn't spare Thuli to come and play with me. She had to help her around the house to cook, clean and look after the baby. The younger girls spent all day collecting fine wood; bring water from the *jhora* in large copper *gagris* which had to be shined before filling with the cool clear water of the *jhora*. They would then carry them up the steep *chorbato* balancing them on their little hips. Then there was washing to do at the *jhora* and looking after the babies that arrived in quick succession year after year. Little girls had no time for fun and frolic, they had no childhood. They become adult housewives straight from childhood.

The boys on the other hand were not allotted any household chores. Those whose fathers could afford the Rs. 2 per month fee, went to school in town while others worked as coolies, ran wild in the mountains and woods. Thuli's *amma* couldn't spare her daughters so she sent her two sons along with their friends to play with me. Ma was taken aback to see the barefooted, dust laden ragged lot with runny noses.

The boys had come armed with a large green *pumelo*, their football. They knew that Monjula had two large fields, not available in the vicinity, ideal for a game of football. I was horrified, how was I supposed to play with these little devilish ruffians? As soon as ma disappeared into the house, with shrieks of pleasure they descended on ma's pristine, green, well manicured lawn, her pride and joy. Four large stones were hastily laid on either end to serve as goal posts and a game of football started in real earnest with the heavy unwieldy *pumelo*.

I held my breath as I stood alone on the front verandah and watched them helplessly, wondering when ma would come out firing on all cylinders and put a stop to the destruction of her prized lawn. Ma did come out and saw me standing alone. "Why aren't you playing with them, after all they have come to play with you?" she asked. I was relieved that I wouldn't be blamed for ruining her precious lawn so in I jumped into the fray.

I didn't know anything about the game of football. The boys realizing this promptly made me a goalkeeper. This was not difficult as I could use my hands, legs and body to stop the *pumelo* from entering between the two rocks, the goal posts. It was too slow and heavy to slide past me unawares. The goalie at the other end was Patal. A short, dark fellow rather hard of hearing but with sharp eyes catching every *pamelo* that came his way. He was virtually impossible to get past, an impregnable wall. He was therefore assigned this position permanently.

He was much sought after by each team so was his cousin Ganesh, a tall boy with pink cheeks eldest of the lot with swift feet. Once he got the *pumelo* his feet were glued to it. He dribbled to perfection passing every player on the field, reaching the goal post effortlessly and then dodging the goalie to sneak the *pumelo* in. We made sure that Patal and Ganesh were not in the same team as they made a formidable duo and the opposite team wouldn't have a chance against them.

Soon word got around that football was being played at Mitter memsahib's lawn so boys from neighbouring villages even as far as *Chibbo Basti,* started arriving to play. The Suberi boys were in the majority, they dictated terms and conditions. They decided who could join in the game and who couldn't out of the boys, Jetha, Maila, Saila, Kancha who arrived each day. In any case the lawn couldn't hold more than a dozen players at a time.

I soon learnt the intricacies of the game and could play fairly well in any position in the field. It was pure fun yet deadly serious when it came to scoring goals and winning. Often arguments ensured with much swearing, I was well versed in this department having learnt every swear word under Bahadur's tutelage. Swearing like a trooper without raising eyebrows or restriction was a great pleasure, something I couldn't do in school or in genteel company. Being a girl they spared me from the fist fights. I was a very shy child and couldn't make friends easily but I was perfectly at home in their company. Playing football with them was a great pleasure both satisfying and thrilling to score a goal. The adrenaline rush was elating and euphoric.

My friends at the convent found out about the *chokra* boys I played football with. They laughed and sniggered at my choice of friends while the nuns thought playing football was most unlady like and playing with boys downright sinful. In my teens again, I was the solitary girl playing tennis with boys and men in the Kalimpong Tennis Club which was frowned upon by the nuns.

The boys and I were getting tired of kicking the heavy *pumelos* around.

Moreover, the tree was getting denuded of *pumelos* rather quickly; soon there would be none left. The boys were happy to have a playground, now their sights were on a regular football so they coerced me to get one. None of them had any money and neither did I. I was keen to have one but didn't dare to ask ma for such an expensive toy.

The boys persisted with their demand, telling me about the virtues of a leather football until I picked up enough courage to broach the subject to ma gently. To my surprise ma readily agreed. She was happy that I had company every evening and enjoying myself. She had sacrificed her precious lawn for my pleasure so why not a football which was expensive costing Rs. 5.

The leather football arrived with a conical, pink rubber bladder with a long tube. The boys were ecstatic, they touched it, caressed it, ran their little finger tips along the seams that held the oblong pieces of crude untreated cow hide together to form the magical sphere.

The rubber bladder was thrust into the bowels of the football through a slit. They took turns to blow into the bladder through the tube to inflate the stiff unyielding leather until the ball swelled, taking shape, to everyone's glee. The long pink tube, the umbilical cord of the ball, was bent and tied to prevent air from escaping then carefully pushed into the slit of the ball and laced tightly to close the gap. The ball was at last ready.

I marvel at footballs made today with built in bladders with a minute hole to inflate it. But then, the cumbersome intricacies of the whole ritual, of pumping and lacing the ball was a fitting preamble to the much anticipated game.

It was a momentous day when the regular football flew faster, higher than the solid, fat unwieldy *pumelo.* Everyone had to run much faster to control the ball.

Now I was the proud owner of a regular football with a pump and lacer as well. This fact gave me a lot of leverage; I was in a position to dictate terms and conditions to the boys. I decided who could play and who could not. If I was ill or too tired to play the ball was not given to them.

My grandmother visiting us was so perturbed by my possessiveness that she bought the boys another ball with the condition that it would remain in Monjula. This deflated me completely.

The new football was a wonderful change from the *pumelo,* it bounced and flew with the slightest of kicks. With speed and precision it beheaded ma's prized dahlias and gladiolas if not intercepted in time. It bounced onto seedlings flattening them to ma's horror but she did not complain. Her daughter's enjoyment was more important.

The next piece of equipment I longed for was a pair of boots. Not football boots because they were unheard of then but just a pair of leather boots. I broached the subject to ma, "Your shoes are good enough for playing football, the boys play barefooted, they don't even have shoes, why do you need boots?," she asked annoyed at my unreasonable request. Actually I wanted a pair of boots because Bahadur had always longed for them as he considered them the ultimate in footwear. After much coaxing, cajoling and sulking ma agreed to get me a pair of boots.

There were several Chinese shoe shops in Kalimpong. The one favoured by ma was a dark gloomy shoe shop, up a flight of steps, on the Main Road where Angel Hair Dressing Saloon now operates. In the dark interior I found dust laden boots and shoes hanging from wooden beams. Two long wooden benches along the wall for customers to sit on, well polished by umpteen posteriors.

The tall thin Chinese shoe maker took the measurement of both my feet on a piece of paper. Ma did the talking all the time as he got on with the job silently. Ma asked him when the boots would be ready and how much he would charge? He opened his mouth to display a large set of yellow teeth with a gold tooth in the corner. His speech was garbled Hindi with such a heavy Chinese accent that was incomprehensible to me. Ma gathered that the boots would be ready in a month and cost Rs. 10. Since readymade footwear was not available I had no choice but to wait patiently for a whole month.

Exactly one month later ma and I appeared at the shoe shop, without a name. The shoemaker searched for my boots on the dusty shelf. I wished that he would hurry up as the smell of leather in the shop was overpowering. At last they appeared. I slipped them on and tied the laces very tight as they were two sizes too big, as per ma's instructions, so that I wouldn't out grow them too soon. I walked around in them proudly.

I noticed, the right boot was flatter and wider than the left one. My feet were perfectly symmetrical but the boots were not. There was nothing to be done about it. I wore the boots for years. They didn't wear out. They just grew smaller as my feet grew bigger. Subsequent pairs were ordered from the same shop and every pair was mismatched!

The boys admired the boots and kept their distance while tackling me to avoid being stamped by the hard leather soles. I was disappointed to find that although I could shoot the ball harder I couldn't control it very well with my boots. The smooth leather soles slipped on the grass even though the lawn was worn thread bare. Eventually I discarded them altogether and played barefooted to the boys's great relief.

When the football season was over each year, the boys would still come to fly kites with me and play other games according to each season. Cricket was unheard of.

My football fellows did very well for themselves, they all got plum jobs. Ganesh joined the army to every one's disappointment. We were sure he would be a football star.

Saila, his brother got a job in the bank. His cousin Tika joined the elite police forces which guard the VIPs both in India and abroad. Patal had a government job from which he has just retired.

The thatched huts on the hill have been replaced by grand double-storied concrete buildings. I often meet Patal on my walks, we stand and chat. He still remembers all the spectacular catches he took and regrets the misses. For a few minutes we are transported to our carefree happy childhood when we played the game of football together.

The Lady was a Tramp

The monsoons were over, days and nights of incessant rain had given way to bright sunshine, balmy clear days and blue skies, making my spirits soar.

I decided to start the day by making and eating some pop corn. I went to the back verandah of our house, Monjula, to get some corn for that purpose. Rows and rows of dried corn hung on horizontal bamboo poles out of reach of rats and mice.

I plucked off two *bhuttas* from the pole and peeled off the coarse outer covering. I came across skeins of long, brown and golden hair covering the yellow corn. I plucked them off gently and ran my fingers through them. They were smooth, pliable and silky. What use can I put them to I wondered.

The hairs would make a wonderful wig. A beard, yes, they would make a fine beard. A brilliant idea indeed. I swung into action, popcorn forgotten.

I made a pot of glue with water and flour. Shut myself in my room and became a makeup artist. I lathered my face with the thick glue, very carefully stuck the *bhutta* hair all over my face and patted them into place. I used a pair of scissors to trim the straggly brown beard and large moustache.

I covered my short black hair with a cap, stuck some strands of the *bhutta* hair under the cap all around, to show that I had similar hair as my beard. I donned a battered pair of shoes minus laces and donned gloves. My disguise was complete. Any Bollywood makeup artist couldn't have done better! I was proud of my efforts and quite sure no one would be able to recognize me as long as I didn't open my mouth to speak.

Now I was ready to put myself to the test. Ma had gone to the *haat,* being a Saturday. Bahadur, was cooking in the kitchen. He knew me better than anyone else, so why not try him out first?

I went to the front door and knocked loudly on the glass pane. Bahadur appeared at the door and stood staring at me. He looked puzzled and a bit afraid, to see this dubious character although he was used to seeing all kinds of odd characters visiting Monjula. He opened the door slightly ajar ready to shut it if necessary and asked me in broken Hindi what I wanted. I couldn't hold up my amusement any longer, I burst out laughing. "Khuku," he whispered incredulously. "Yes, yes," I cried delighted that I had fooled him. My makeup was fool proof though rather odd.

My next victim was George Patterson who lived next door in Chitrabhanu. I went up to his flat and knocked. Patterson opened the door, his blue eyes showed surprise, then twinkled, he let out a whoop, grabbed my gloved hand and cried, "Monila!" I hadn't spoken a word, yet he had recognized me. I was rather disappointed. "How did you recognize me?" I asked, feeling rather foolish. "Why your pullover, I have seen you in it before."

Who to fool next, why not my friends in St. Joseph's Convent so I walked down to the Convent. I had no idea what I would do there or the reception I would receive. The nuns might set the dogs on me but it turned out to be far more productive than I had ever imagined.

Saturday being a holiday all the kids would be out playing. The best thing would be to approach the playground down the little path that ran down the steep hillside, covered with bushes and trees. I made my way half way down the path. Nobody noticed me so I went further and sat down in full view of the children below. The children were so engrossed in their games that nobody noticed me for quite some time. At last one little girl did. Eyes wide with terror she backed away silently, pointing me out to her friends.

The children huddled around her looking up at me petrified. *"Bhoot, bhoot!"* they kept repeating. The other girls soon joined them. Being bolder and older they crept up closer and closer to the stone wall where the hill slope ended, trying to figure out whether I was a *bhoot,* or not. Once they were sure I was not from the nether world, they relaxed.

Speculation ran high, "A mad man," said one. "No, no, he is not mad, just a poor beggar," said another. "He is a scarecrow; no he is just a tramp." "What an odd looking tramp." "What is he doing here?" Not afraid any more they started shouting and laughing, a bit apprehensive though.

Their numbers grew until all the boarders came to watch the tramp on the hillside. I waved at them and nodded my head sending them into peals of laughter. I tried to smile too but the glue on my face had hardened and I couldn't open my mouth, making the moustache and the beard permanent. The girls laughed, screamed in mock horror every time I made some motion. They were highly amused by my antics.

The teacher on duty tried to draw the children away from their new pastime but to no avail. They refused to go and play. The young teachers living in the teacher's quarters appeared one by one to see what the commotion was all about. They couldn't quite figure out who this strange looking person was perched on the hillside or what he wanted.

Next arrived the august and last line of resistance, the nuns, Mother Cecelia, Mother Teresa and Mother John Mary. The teacher on duty ran around helter skelter, red in the face trying to control the children from making the most atrocious noise.

Suddenly Mother's Cecelia's strong, deep voice boomed. "Attay, Attay, go up there and see what that man wants, tell him to go away at once."

Attay was the handy, strong man of the Convent. Well built, young, fearless but deaf and dumb. Mother Cecilia pointed me out to him and shoved him off. Attay realized his mission and ran up the little path towards me. As he came nearer to me his pace decreased until he stood stock still, just ten yards from me. I waved at him. All his strength and bravado deserted him. He just turned tail and fled as if he had seen a real *bhoot.*

There was pin drop silence down below as Attay had made his way up, expecting some positive action from him and reaction from me. But the minute he fled the children broke out into shrill, uncontrollable laughter. Attay, the superman, their hero had failed to oust me from my perch so now I became their hero. They cheered, clapped their hands and their united voices grew into a crescendo.

The nuns and teachers ran around like puppets, red in the face shouting, "Quiet! Quiet!" trying to quell the exuberant girls without effect. They had turned into a jumping, thumping, shouting, hysterical mass. I was quite shocked to see them in this state. I didn't realise that I was just the catalyst that had triggered off this eruption of frenzy.

They had been sedate young ladies far too long. Their pent up emotions, energy, childish exuberance had been curbed with no outlet at all. Under strict supervision and surveillance they had become lifeless zombies. It was drilled into them that it was unlady like to shout, scream, talk loudly or show any emotion until they had stopped being natural high spirited children. It was lady like to be demure, soft spoken, gentle and obedient. The rules were endless, discipline rigid.

This was their chance to break all rules and regulations, give free rein to their pent up feelings and just let their hair down for once. They knew full well that no one could be singled out for this outrageous behaviour and punished. Why not go all the way then and enjoy themselves. The noise they made turned into a deafening roar penetrating every room of the huge school building. The nuns in the chapel in deep prayer wondered what hell had broken loose.

I decided it was time to go home but I was not going to slink away quietly as I had come. I had to show the girls who the tramp really was. They would never believe me if I told them on Monday that it was me up on the hill dressed as a tramp. They would make fun of me and I would never be able to live down their jibes and my humiliation.

I was shy, quiet, diminutive, a model child well-liked by the teachers and nuns. A nonentity, just a face in the crowd. What started off as an insignificant prank had unleashed a pandemonium unsurpassed in the history of the school till this day.

I was not going to let this opportunity go by, to prove I had done the unattainable. I had driven the whole school berserk and no one had recognized me. No mean feat that!

It was now or never. I had to show them it was me, in flesh and blood. It was my day, I had to win kudos. It was a matter of do or die. After all I hadn't broken any rules, I hadn't harmed anybody so why not go down to the play-ground and expose myself?

I got up and made my way down the path, there was a sudden hush, I saw a sea of scared faces receding. Girls tumbling over each other to get as far away from me as possible. At the end of the path, in the most dramatic pose I could muster, I flung off my cap and with a flourish, tore off my beard crying "Ha! Ha! Ha!" in real filmy style.

Hundreds of eyes stared at me spell bound as my black hair came tumbling down and a portion of my beard fell off. There was stunned silence, then, once they recognized me, they came bounding up to grab and hug me. Pleasure and admiration writ large on their glowing happy faces. "It was you all the time," they cried mobbing me, each one vying to clasp my hands as if I was a great celebrity, a pop star.

I had never expected this joyous reception; it was beyond my wildest dream. Reverend mother Phillip, the principal, came up to me. Her ever calm, pious face livid and asked me "I can't believe that you can do such a disgraceful thing, to come dressed like a tramp and disturb the whole school. I am ashamed of you. Does your mother know about this?" I shook my head completely defeated. "I must let her know about this."

With that she stomped off angrily with a swish of her long habit and rattling rosary. I hung down my head in mortification. I had never been scolded by any teacher, except Bosie so far, leave alone the Reverend Mother, that too, in front of the whole school and thoroughly disgraced. It was most unexpected.

After all it was a simple prank, a harmless joke which didn't deserve the wrath of the gentle Reverend Mother who never raised her voice. Her stately figure, cool, calm, firm voice was enough to keep any child from repeating the same mistake twice. This was the only time anybody saw her lose her cool.

We were all stunned by her sudden outburst and I wished the play ground would open up and swallow me.

Later I learnt why she had lost her temper with me. As luck would have it, the 5th standard children were sitting for a board examination that day. They were sitting in the study hall next to the playground. It was not an important exam. But it was going to bring prestige to the school if the children did well.

The ruckus on the play ground disturbed them thoroughly. All the windows had been shut to keep out the noise but the children could see the fun and games going on outside through the large window panes. They longed to join the others outside rather than answer the stupid question paper. They couldn't care less how they performed in this silly exam. It was a useless exercise they thought so they put down their pens and watched with glee what was going on outside. They just couldn't concentrate. So this is what gave rise to Reverend Mother's ire. I had chosen the wrong day.

Reverend Mother never wrote to ma about my unlady like bad behaviour. Well ma's sense of humour was certainly much greater than Reverend Mother's, she roared with laughter when she heard about the episode from one of the teachers.

This happened many years ago but I had made an impression alright. Whenever I meet anybody in any part of the world today who was present, that day, in the Convent, remembers me as the most amusing tramp.

This has been an oft repeated story, told to the children by their mothers, who had enjoyed the antics of the tramp that day at the Convent. Now I tell it to my grandson who never tires of hearing it.

Prince Charming

As a child, I could never figure out how he could be the Prince of Greece and Denmark, of two countries lying at opposite ends of Europe moreover, he did not fit the description of the fairy tale prince I was always reading about. No regal attire or any other symbol, to differentiate him from the ordinary foreigner. Royal blue blood coursed through his veins I was told. He was related to Lord Mountbatten, Prince Philip and several royal families of Europe.

His Royal highness Prince Peter of Greece and Denmark, a tall well built, middle aged man had no airs about him. He mixed freely with one and all without reservations while his commoner wife, Princess Irene, a stickler for protocol, remained aloof. She lived in her ivory tower and perhaps out of boredom, wrote a voluminous book on witch craft.

The Prince, a good conversationalist with a sense of humour was friendly and approachable. A simple man but his life style was far from simple, it was princely.

The first house he lived in Kalimpong was Tashiding in Rinkingpong. A British style house, complete with stables full of horses, large well trained domestic staff from gardeners to butlers, a foreign personal secretary, a cellar full of foreign vintage wine and a bar full of choicest drinks.

Being an anthropologist, he spent hours at the Tibetan muleteer's camps just outside Kalimpong, studying the Tibetan muleteers's behaviour, habits and backgrounds. Measuring their arms, legs and skull sizes etc. Material for his forth coming book.

The general public maintained that he was a spy gleaning information from the muleteers coming out of the forbidden land, Tibet. At that time there were vague rumors floating around about invasion of Tibet by the Chinese.

There was an old, long arduous trade route from Lhasa to Kalimpong in those days, mules being the only means of transport through the treacherous mountain terrain. The muleteers a rough, tough, hardy lot led their mules carrying huge, heavy loads back and forth. Under such a political climate who would know more about what was happening in isolated Tibet than these simple, illiterate muleteers. They were the only source of information, however, vague and unsubstantial their reports might be.

What added weight to these rumors was the fact that the Prince had appointed a few learned Tibetans to teach him Tibetan! This would enable him to converse directly with muleteers without the help of an incompetent interpreter.

Nobody, of course knew whom he was spying for or why. Nobody cared or bothered about such things, it only lent more colour to his flamboyant character. For us children, it lent more than colour, fired our fertile childish imagination. I and my friends were in awe of the Prince in disguise, bereft of his royal attire and trappings, mingling freely with all and sundry to spy. We were determined to find out his secret mission, expose him and become famous detectives like Enid Blyton's, "Famous Five."

Betty and I schemed and plotted to catch him red handed. This meant action. So action it was. We decided the perfect time to invade his house would be the afternoon. Going out at night was out of the question.

Afternoon was siesta time, the servants would safely be out of the way in their quarters and we would have a clear field to spy on a spy!

We made our way into his compound through a gap in the hedge, not through the wide open main gate. There was not a soul in sight. Perfect silence greeted us. We got bolder, circled the house, still no one. We tried all the doors and windows, everything was tightly shut. Now, I wonder what we would have done if we had found an access to the house. We didn't have the faintest idea of what we were looking for.

The curtains were not drawn. So with our noses flattened on the glass panes we gazed in wonder at the splendor of each room. The rooms were all beautifully and tastefully decorated with elegant furniture, thick rich carpets, rare *Thankas,* paintings, gleaming crystals and silver. Luckily, our invasion of his privacy went undetected. We couldn't venture any further. Just as well.

In those days nobody locked their doors and windows but the Prince did. Obviously he had something to hide. "What?" was the million dollar question. There was no way to find out, so rather dejected, we wound our way to the main gate. Parked right next to the gate, under a make shift awning, stood the most enormous van we had ever seen. Shining, pale green, large as a house, stood the van on massive jet-black tyres. Curiosity got the better of us.

Climbing on the high foot board we inspected the innards of the van. There were no seats in the van except for the driver's seat; instead there were two narrow beds, a tiny toilet with a commode and basin. A kitchen with astove, sink and cupboards, everything in miniature. What a perfect setting for paying our favourite game house, house. The highlight of our spying mission turned out to be the van, not the spy. To this day I clearly remember every detail of that beautiful caravan.

Prince Peter was a frequent guest at our house Monjula for tea. Once I was surprised to find him standing just outside our gate when I returned home from school on horseback. I wished him and rode in. He made no move to follow me. Intrigued I reported this to ma. She looked at the clock and smiled. "You see, it is not 4'o clock yet. I have invited him for tea at 4 p.m. He will not come in until 4." Sure enoug he breezed in at the dot of 4 p.m.

The prince was often invited by ma but his wife never accompanied him although, she was most cordially invited. She appeared to be perpetually indisposed. She never socialised or attended any parties. The only time she attended a coffee party was when Pandit Nehru visited Kalimpong. The ladies of Kalimpong had organized a coffee morning for him. Princess Irene was also invited.

Nobody expected her to turn up but she did, in her latest Paris outfit with a lustrous string of gleaming pearls as large as marbles, around her neck. Pandit Nehru enjoying the party suddenly pointed to the Princess's pearls with his eyes and whispered to ma in Hindi "Are those pearls real?" ma whispered back, "A princess can't be wearing fake pearls."

One day a Russian family of three arrived in Kalimpong from Tibet. They had lived in Tibet for generations but the Chinese invasion of Tibet forced them to flee. Mother, Father and their teenage daughter had made their way, by the trade route, from Tibet to Kalimpong with the muleteers. The treacherous and difficult route through the Himalayas had taken its toll. They arrived in a foreign land penniless, with only their tattered clothes on their backs, mentally and physically exhausted.

Prince Peter found them in the muleteer's camp, cold, hungry and depressed. He brought the trio home immediately and gave them food and shelter. They were very poor, simple people, could only speak Tibetan and a smattering of Russian. As they grew healthier and stronger the Prince absorbed them in his household.

The man was put in charge of the stables. The woman to do domestic chores and their daughter, Tania, was sent to my school, Saint Joseph's Convent as a boarder, to receive education. The Russian couple flourished in the Prince's household. Security and kindness brought back their confidence, they learnt to live without fear once more and smile again.

In school we took a long time to get used to Tania and her rustic background and vice versa. A very fair, tall, thin awkward teenager she was uncomfortable in her smart, new school uniform. She looked terrified and unhappy with her face screwed up perpetually and unknown fear in her blue eyes.

We were very curious to learn about her past, something she didn't want to remember. We couldn't converse with her anyway. She could only speak Tibetan and the only Tibetan word we knew was "*Mindu.*" Her surname was a real tongue twister so we christened her Tania *Mindu.* Soon all the teachers and nuns started referring to her as Tania *Mindu.*

Although a teenager and older than us, we found her very childish. The Princess, on one of her rare visits to the market, had taken Tania with her. Tania's eyes had lit up at the sight of a doll in a shop. She insisted on having it. Since that day, it became her constant companion. The silent companionship of the inanimate doll must have been more reassuring and comforting than a band of demanding, leg-pulling, alien, insensitive school girls.

Long ago I had given up all childish activities of spy hunts. Now I concentrated and devoted all my energies on more positive and physical exercise like tennis rather than imaginary ones.

The first time the Prince really noticed me was when I beat him at a game of tennis one afternoon in the Kalimpong tennis club. The Prince was full of praise. I was thrilled and elated. It made my day. Coming to think of that win now, I am convinced that being the perfect gentleman that he was, he deliberately lost to me.

The outcome of this game of tennis was an invitation to accompany ma, for the first time, to his house for lunch. No child was ever invited to his house so I felt very special. I reminded myself that I was not a child any more but a teenager.

We arrived at his new residence, Krishna Lodge for lunch. The beautifully tended garden was full of exotic flowers. At one end of the garden stood heavy wrought iron garden furniture from Spain. Each room slid out of pages of a glossy magazine so did slim, tall Princess Irene in an haute couture summer dress. A lady of very few words but a perfect hostess. That was the first and last time I met her.

I was nervous and tongue tied in such august and adult company. The Prince sensing my discomfort, very casually alighted on subjects that interested a teenager. Soon I was perfectly at ease and felt very much at home. There were several other guests at the party too.

Lunch was announced and we trooped into the long, dimly lit dining room and were seated at table according to the place marked for each. The long highly polished mahogany dining table held a dazzling array of crockery, cutlery, a battery of crystal wine glasses but most eye catching of all was the centre piece. A gorgeous thick bed of brilliant yellow flowers lay on a large rectangular mirror lit up by a single beam of light directly focused at it from the ceiling. The effect was stunning.

The bearer approached, holding a wine bottle wrapped in a white napkin in his gloved hand, for the Prince to taste and give his approval. Approval given, the bearer started pouring the golden, sparkling liquid into each guest's crystal glass. This was not the first time I saw wine and longed to taste it but ma said "No" and when my turn came I too had to say "No", reluctantly. A different wine appeared with each course. Now the deep, dark, wine sparkled as it fell into another glass.

I can't remember the exact number or names of the dishes we ate but I remember the food being delicious, delicate and dainty. Meat, fish delectable delicacies, all exotic ingredients were flown in from Calcutta each week and stored in the refrigerator. Theirs was the sole fridge in Kalimpong in those days.

The Prince bought the large stone house, made it fit for a Prince and called it Krishna Lodge, in memory of his dearly beloved pet squirrel called Krishna. The Prince and Krishna shared a very special friendship. He would happily ride on the Prince's shoulder everywhere he went. He would scamper down and hide in the Prince's shirt pocket if danger threatened or just take a nap quietly if the company the Prince was keeping proved too boring. Krishna would travel in the plane to Calcutta perched on his royal shoulder making eyes at the air hostesses. The Prince was devastated when Krishna died.

The house now is dead too, burnt down during the Gorkhaland movement. If only the burnt down walls could speak, they would tell you about gracious living, ambiance of an era gone by when Prince Charming lived in it.

White Mouse

In the fifties, the obscure little town of Kalimpong, saw an influx of foreigners from all parts of the world. Their sole purpose of being here was to learn Tibetan. The general public branded them as spies. Pandit Nehru stated that Kalimpong was "A nest of spies."

They were all middle aged or young, so everybody was curious when the elderly gentleman, Mr. Roc, arrived with a young secretary in tow, with no particular purpose in mind. He looked a hard boiled business man with a shining pate, horn-rimmed spectacles with thick lenses, always in a brown business suit. He was far from friendly.

His young Austrian secretary Dr. Rene Nebesky, still wet under the gills, had accompanied him, lured by a substantial pay packet and all expenses paid deal. Dr. Rene nebesky became very famous after he went back to Austria from Kalimpong years later and wrote a very comprehensive book on the Lepchas. He turned out to be a highly respected scholar of great repute in the western world.

The two took up residence at the Himalayan Hotel. All the foreigners converged there. In the evenings they sat in the drawing room to socialize and down glasses of beer. Annie Perry, Queen of Ceremonies, friendly and charming, regaled them with interesting stories. She not only made them feel at home but became their friend and guide. She was the life and soul of the hotel.

The young guests mostly bachelors, were very excited when a well stacked young lady arrived at the hotel, claiming to be Henrick Harrar's sister, Lydia. I remember her as just stunning! She had not come to learn Tibetan but to meet her famous brother who was on his way to Kalimpong from Tibet. The young men vied for her attention every evening. The crusty old man Mr. Roc, not to be left out of the fray, started wooing her with adour. Unfortunately, his virile young secretary very quickly made more headway in that direction.

On a full moon night, Mr. Roc invited Nebesky for a walk not a duel! As the moon climbed higher so did Mr. Roc's temper. Without rhyme or reason he started abusing Nebesky. His whole body shook with rage. His flabby body shook like jelly, his flushed face as full as the moon was red with rage. He walked on unsteady legs, shaking his fists in frenzy. Nebesky was sure the moon had affected him and turned him into a raging lunatic. He managed to coax and cajole Mr. Roc back to the hotel and into bed. The next morning when Nebesky woke up, Mr. Roc was gone.

Nebesky was in a quandary. Miles away from home in a foreign land with no job, no money. He cursed his luck and the day he had set eyes on Lydia. Her illustrious brother never arrived so she left, leaving behind a string of admirers with broken hearts.

Prince Peter hearing about Nebesky's plight came to his rescue with alacrity. Nebesky had an authentic doctorate in anthropology. Just the right man to help him with his forth coming book on that very subject. The Prince appointed Nebesky as his personal secretary for the princely sum of Rs. 100 per month, without board and lodging.

Ma, the patron saint of the distressed, offered to give free board and lodging to Nebesky until he could fend for himself. This was impossible on Rs. 100 per month so instead of a few days, as originally envisaged, he became almost a permanent fixture in our out house, Monjula ii.

Soon, the blond, lanky young man indulged by ma, out grew his only grey suit. Ma promptly knitted him a pullover. Ma became his *didi,* as he very easily and happily settled down in Monjula taking her kindness and hospitality for granted.

The servants took to him too and affectionately called him *Sayto Musa*! in Nepali. The reason being his blond hair, white eyebrows and skin; as for his name, it was an absolute tongue twister, so *'Sayto Musa,'* it was.

I had a couple of pet guinea pigs in a pen. They too, were called *'Sayto Musa,'* for the lack of a distinguishing name for them in Nepali. Nebesky was very fond of these guinea pigs. every day he would stop by their pen to feed them tidbits and talk to them affectionately.

Nebesky was the only child of doting, elderly parents who wrote to him regularly so did his relatives and friends. He waited patiently for these letters every day. They were his lifeline to sanity, in his alien solitary confinement.

Bahadur, had left us for greener pastures but came to meet me often. One afternoon, he arrived with a bunch of letters the postman had handed him for Monjula. I glanced through the letters and found they were all for Nebesky. "Oh, they are all for *'Sayto Musa,'* go and give them to him." He gave me a puzzled look and asked, "Do *Sayto Musas,* eat paper?" "*Musa*s eat everything, don't you know?" I flung back and went off to play, not realizing that this man did not know Nebesky's pet name.

That evening we were startled by loud cries of pain and anger followed by anguished cries of, "*Didi*! *Didi*! Please come *didi*!" We all ran out expecting to find Nebesky strangled or stabbed, in throes of death, crying for help with his last breath. There he was kneeling by the guinea pig's pen, his white face tomato red, shaking uncontrollably. "Look *didi*, look," he screamed. "These are my letters in the pen, who put them there?" Sure enough, half eaten picture post cards with foreign stamps, air-mail letters with serrated edges and envelops with holes lay scattered in the pen.

The guinea pigs sleeping blissfully in their boxes, after the unusual but tasty meal of foreign stationery, were rudely woken up by loud noises. The noises were emanating from the very individual who always fed them and spoke to them gently. Terrified and confused they shriveled up into tight balls and stared at him with their beady, black eyes, terror stricken.

I fled into the house bursting with laughter as soon I realized what had happened here. Ma cornered me soon, suspecting that I had a hand in the guinea pig's unusual meal. I told her what I suspected with as straight a face as I could muster.

Ma's sense of humour prevailed as she saw the funny side of the whole episode and I was not blamed for any misadventure! She had to give Nebesky some explanation for the jig-saw puzzle his letters had turned into.

"Rene," she began soothingly, "You know Bahadur? Well, he had collected the letters from the postman today and for some unknown reason he left them in the guinea pig's pen." she finished lamely.

"What! that man must have been drunk, no mad, a mad man." he screamed. Well Nebesky had firsthand experience of illogical mad men. He put nothing past them.

Every evening Nebesky would keep us and all our guests, at dinner, well entertained with his war time exploits. Hair raising stories of narrow escapes, blowing up enemy property, tanks, saving lives and furious gun battles. In short he was one of those unsung, unrecognized war heroes. He achieved the desired result; he became a super hero in our eyes.

The year was nearly over. *Kali puja,* my favourite festival of lights had arrived. Every year, friends came on this day to Monjula for high tea and fireworks display. I am very fond of rockets, flower pots, sparklers but not ear splitting bombs and crackers but they were bought all the same as the servants insisted on having them, to chase away evil spirits. To please them, bombs arrived in all shapes and sizes. Big ones, little ones and tiny ones plaited together which went off in sequence.

Highly satisfied with the sumptuous high tea, bellies brimming over, guests along with Nebesky lolled on cane chairs on the verandah for the fireworks to begin.

Bahadur, always present on such occasions, helped me to light the *diyas* and sparklers. His job too was to handle the bombs and crackers. He was not satisfied with the bombs. "They are not loud enough and the little ones are flying all over the place." he grumbled.

Always innovative, he asked for a steel bucket, put the little plaited bombs under the upside down bucket, on the hard cemented surface of the verandah and lighted them. What followed would have earned him an Oscar for sound effect!

The first explosion in the close confines of the heavy bucket boomed like cannon fire, followed by rat-a-tat of an automatic rifle as the little bombs went off in sequence. The flickering *diyas* and the roaring bonfire in the middle of the lawn presented a perfect battle scene.

I clapped my hands in glee but my happiness was short lived. Terrified screams rose from the verandah. Nebesky, arms flailing wildly, face contorted in intense agony, eyes bulging with fear, thrashed round on his chair, finally finding his feet, he shot through the nearest door into the drawing room. All the evil spirits seemed to have converged on him with a vengeance.

Ma, along with the alarmed guests, rushed in behind him. He lay on the divan reduced to a blabbing, dithering idiot. No amount of consoling or buckets of cold water could calm his shattered nerves. Then doctor Boral was called. After examining the patient, he gave his diagnosis, "Shell shock,"he declared gravely!

The Princess

Rumours, whispered in the dim corridors of St. Joseph's Convent were that Mother John Mary, the slim slight and unassuming nun was a princess. Each new batch of students who were old enough to understand the magnitude of this information held her in awe.

It was difficult to believe that this old nun with sharp, deep set eyes, thin lips and aquiline nose was a princess. By no stretch of imagination was it possible to imagine her as a daintily dressed, doe eyed princess in her long, flowing gown, golden slippers and a diamond-studded tiara on her head full of golden hair. To our childish eyes, she appeared more like a sharpe eyed eagle with black feathers.

We hardly saw or knew her as she flitted quietly in the background until we came in contact with her in the last year of school, in the Senior Cambridge class. She was our class teacher. She was different from all the other teachers we had encountered so far.

She was calm, quiet, soft-spoken and gentle. She never scolded us or raised her voice. A perfect lady, always in control of her emotions. She treated us like young ladies and we in turn respected her and never did anything to displease her.

Highly intelligent, Mother had mastery over every subject she taught us. She explained each lesson to us calmly and precisely and made them interesting. We learned them effortlessly. The subjects that bored us earlier and we had studied just for passing exams. were coming alive now. We were acquiring knowledge at last. We gave her our full and undivided attention. Actually, we had no scope for day-dreaming or any other form of distraction as we all sat under her very nose.

We not only took great interest in all that she taught us but suddenly everyone wanted to excel, just to please her. Her words of praise, for a piece of work well done, were few and far between and very difficult to elicit. But when they came, we were elated. It was like winning the bumper prize in a lottery.

Although, Mother was a master of all subjects, her favorite subjects were Geography, Literature and Composition. She generated such an interest in me in Geography and Composition that I excelled in both these subjects and that brought the slightest of smiles to her thin lips.

Mother was determined to educate us. Just book-learning and getting through exams. Was no good. There was a purpose behind every subject which seemed irrelevant to us then. Her objective was to enrich our lives, make us knowledgeable and educated. She would stray away from our curriculum and text to broaden our minds, to develop our taste, to enjoy the inner and deeper elements and appreciate finer things of life.

So she would not give us the usual type of subjects required by the examiners to write essays on but a variety of difficult, obscure topics.

These subjects required full concentration and abundance of imagination, flow of correct grammatical sentences, well-chosen words and epithets to express thoughts, feelings and emotions clearly. Very soon we learnt grammar, the bug bear of the English language, spelling, construction of sentences, punctuation, new words and ways to express ourselves precisely.

Literature too was not spared by her enthusiasm to take us to the realms that would enable us to appreciate the work of great authors. She adhered to the prescribed texts but every afternoon she would read to us wonderful short stories or excerpts from books of famous authors. These afternoon sessions she enjoyed as much as we did. In the process, she achieved her goal; we started reading and appreciating books of the great masters instead of the childish school girl books. She had instilled, in at least some of us, the joys of reading and embracing books as our greatest companions for the rest of our lives.

Mother was in charge of the little library in our school. She doled out the books once a week. She knew exactly what each child was reading. She never interfered with a child's choice of books. They were all very simple, harmless books. Books with the slightest hint of love or romance were not kept in the library and such books were strictly banned in the school premises.

My friend Elsie, a book worm and eternal romantic, persuaded me to bring her a few juicier books from home. Being a boarder, she did not have access to such books. I obliged and gave her three very innocent but spicy books to read. She read them surreptitiously in bed, under the blanket by torch light, in the toilet or in the study hall. She would pretend to be doing her homework very diligently with all her books spread out on the top of the desk while the story book lay open on her lap below.

She managed to evade detection so far but Mother John Mary's sharp eyes finally caught her. She caught Elise reading the books in the study hall. She confiscated them at once without a word of reprimand or trying to find out the source of the books. Elsie felt guilty and was chastised for breaking the school rule without a single word of reproach from Mother. She returned the books to Elsie eventually.

This was Mother's greatest asset. She never uttered a harsh word, never scolded or humiliated anyone. The slightest sign of disapproval on her gentle face was enough to embarrass and stop a child from repeating her misdeed. Accusing or punishing anyone was completely alien to her nature. She treated us not like earring, naughty children but as responsible young adults and in return she received our love, loyalty and respect.

She was kind, gentle and ladylike, a perfect Princess. While Mother was on her voyage of educating us in all aspects of life, we grew restless and worried. We were determined to pass our Senior Cambridge exams. At the end of the year.

We were only eager to stick to our syllabuses. We grumbled, fretted and fumed about Mother's deviation from the syllabus. Although, we enjoyed the interesting diversions Mother subjected us to but we were doubly anxious. We were least bothered about Mother's ambition to send us out as well mannered, well turned out, knowledgeable, smart young ladies of poise, grace and charm.

Mother took great pains to correct our garbled speech. Each word had to be precise and clear. This she achieved by making us read all our lessons out loud. Lessons were punctuated by hints on etiquette and manners.

Mother understood each child's problem very well and always tried to solve it. Once Elizabeth's hand turned black and blue because of constant encounter with the ruler wielded by a sadistic teacher. The reason: Elizabeth couldn't fathom the intricacies of Mathematics. Mother was distressed at the teacher's inhuman teaching methods and promptly transferred Elizabeth to another class to save her from further torture and humiliation.

Mother loved birds, animals even frogs. We were always up to our usual tricks in the classroom in the absence of Mother. Once during lunch break, I brought a nice, fat, full grown frog and deposited it inside my friend Pramila's desk. She was the only one, not present, in the classroom at that time. We were looking forward to some fun at her expenses once she returned. Unfortunately, she came back rather late and Mother appeared earlier than usual for the afternoon session.

Everybody in the class except Pramila, knew about the frog inside her desk. Mother started reading a very interesting story as usual. For once, nobody was paying any attention to the story, except Pramila. Everybody's mind was on the frog in her desk. We were fervently praying for the Literature class to finish and the art class to begin. The short gap between change of teachers would give us a chance to warn Pramila of what was in her desk and not to open it.

We held our breath as Pramila, for some unknown reason, suddenly opened the top flap of her desk quickly to take out something. Her whole head was inside the desk. She did not see the frog right away and was about to close the flap when she saw it. She gave the slightest of gasps and shut the flap quickly.

We heaved a sigh of relief. Good girl, she had not made a scene. But her eyes had opened wide with shock and terror.

We admired her self control, but who would dare to create a scene in Mother's quiet, calm dignified presence.

Mother, however, noticed her terror-stricken eyes. "What is the matter Pramila, are you feeling unwell?" she asked concerned. "Nothing Mother," Pramila replied in a whisper. "Well, something must be wrong, what is it?"

"Mother, there is a frog in my desk!" she stuttered. I was quaking in my shoes. There will be fireworks now, I thought. The culprit would be made to own up to her misdeed and punished. I would have to take the rap. What bad luck!

Mother hurried over from her table and opened Pramila's desk. Pramila was too petrified to move. Mother saw the frog crawling in one corner. She picked it up gently and walked out of the classroom, muttering about insensitivity and cruelty.

We watched her through the window as she appeared in the garden below. She carefully put the frog down on a soft flower bed, in its natural surroundings and freedom. She came right back after completing her mission of mercy. Sat down and carried on reading from where she had left off, as if nothing unusual had happened and no interruption had taken place.

We marveled at her composure, tolerance and insight into childish behaviour. There was no lengthy inquisition, no singling out of the culprit, punishment and humiliation. She was only sorry and upset about the mishandling of the frog and its confinement in the desk. Her dignified and casual handling of the incident made me feel more guilty and embarrassed than any punishment she could have meted out to me. I was fittingly chastised without a single would being uttered.

Mother always stayed behind the scenes. But we were lucky to be in constant touch with her for nine months of our lives. She spent a lot of time in the chapel praying, doing penance on her knees with arms outstretched. A pious and holy person, a living saint in our eyes. We felt privileged to have come in such close contact with her and had got to know her.

I could never fathom why a Princess had renounced her kingdom, given up an easy life of luxury and chosen a life of hardship to serve God and humanity? Was it a calling or was she unlucky in love? Whatever the reason she served God faithfully and left a lasting impression on everyone she came in touch with. We did her proud by passing our Senior Cambridge exam. It was our humble offering to her. When she read the results, a fleeting smile hovered on her thin lips, and her sharp, deep set eyes lit up.

Very recently, I heard that she was not a Princess at all but the daughter of the Governor of the Philippines. The information is irrelevant to me. She always acted and behaved like a true Princess. We never doubted that she was anything but a Princess.

The Master Craftsman

Rows of bared teeth, seven pairs of black eyeless sockets stared at me menacingly from seven smooth white skulls. I drew back in horror and fright. The *coolies,* standing around them gravely, looked frightened too. They had unearthed seven fully intact skeletons from shallow graves while preparing the site for a new building about to be constructed, next door to our house Monjula. After much contemplation they decided to rebury the skeletons in a deeper grave exactly where they found them to lie in peace forever.

No, this was not genocide or the handiwork of a Blue Beard. This area, long forgotten a defunct burial ground was taken over by the British in a bid to develop Kalimpong and sold as building plots.

The house that was built on of this plot was meticulously planned and designed by Rathindranath Tagore, the only son of Rabindranath Tagore and presented to his wife Protima Tagore who named it Chitrabhanu. The house was completed in 1943 and we were invited to the *Grihaprabesh.* Rathibabu, as he was popularly known, proudly took us on a guided tour of his very original magnificent house.

In love with nature, the building was created to blend in with nature surrounding it. The walls were of hand hewn dark grey stones, the roof of asbestos, constructed in steps of several elevations and angles to fit rooms of various sizes and shapes below. The first floor rooms did not sit squarely on top of the ground floor but at the far end. An elevation perfectly designed to break up the monotony of the usual square block. The outward view, a perfect blend of subtle shapes, pleasing to the eye.

He had never studied architecture yet created a masterpiece.

The interior of the house was a perfect union of western comfort in superb Indian design. He had used wood abundantly. Wooden floors, panels, light shades, fittings and fixtures proclaimed his lifelong romance with wood.

Each piece of furniture was unique. The shapes, sizes, lines, Indian motifs but British in character. Natural colours of wood used not only for inlays but in furniture to enhance the lines and designs. The humble wooden pelmets expressed their individuality so did ordinary brackets, doors, windows. They all bore his special stamp of originality and refined taste.

Every morning Rathibabu, in his usual shapeless long robe, like Rabindranath's, walked around in his stone walled garden. The garden too, was perfectly planned and laid out by him. The wall was shaped with alcoves and seats, at various elevations, depending on the amount of privacy required by people who used them.

Wooden trellises, pergolas for creepers covered one side of the garden. A heart shaped lily pool with gold fish, lay below the portrait of Rabindranath with his famous couplet "My joy abounds in sound and colour of this day. Is Kalimpong aware of it?" A stone pillared arbour with a canopy of bougainvillea, over looked Atisha Road below. Narrow gravel paths bordered by neat flower bed criss-crossed the garden in perfect geometrical patterns.

Every summer and *pujas,* the Tagores arrived from Shantiniketan for a prolonged stay in Kalimpong with a large entourage of servants. Two expert cooks. One prepared European dishes solely for Rathibabu, a man with a weak constitution. The other prepared special Tagore family recipes for guests. A valet for the master and an ayah for the mistress. A number of servants meant for specific jobs, a marketing manager cum supervisor and an attendant for the dogs.

This band of well trained, highly paid, uniformed servants walked out en masse one day, after an altercation with the marketing manager. They spent the whole day going from house to house seeking employment. That evening they trooped back sheepishly as nobody in Kalimpong could afford them.

Rathibabu was very fond of dogs. He had a pair of handsome highly pedigreed golden retrievers. Once a litter of thirteen pups were born, two days, before Mr. And Mrs. Tagore's departure for Kalimpong from Shatiniketan. These precious bundles couldn't be left behind so they travelled with them most comfortably in the train, in a large cushioned basket. The puppies were delightful and I spent many an hour playing with them.

Protima Devi was the personification of her name. A raving beauty in her youth, she still retained her lily white flawless skin, an abundance of jet black hair, parted in the middle forming a large *khopa* at the back of her head. She was not only beautiful outwardly but inwardly as well. Soft spoken, ever so gentle, refined and cultured she won all hearts with generous doses of love and kindness. She became ma's best friend and all of us loved her dearly.

She had been her father-in-law's, Rabindranath's favourite. He not only groomed her perfectly to carry on the famous Tagore family tradition but tutored her about his boundless literature and songs until she became an authority on his literary works. At all soirees she chose the most appropriate songs, poems depending on the season, mood and company from her vast knowledge and familiarity with his works.

Rathibabu a tall dark, handsome, silent man with brushed back thinning white hair, rimless glasses was not overly enthusiastic about his illustrious father's sublime literature nor did he inherit an iota of his literary genius. But then Rabindranaths are not born every day. Once in a millennium perhaps, or never again.

Being the only son of his famous father he must have found it very difficult to carry the burden of his father's name and fame. That too, for not making any contribution of his own in that department. He appeared less than mediocre in comparison but he was a geniusin his own right, own field, where his real interest lay. He had refused to go to England for further studies but went to Japan instead, with my father, then to America to study agriculture.

Every morning after breakfast, he would sit at his work table, in a little passage behind the dining room and start his carpentry. His only passion in life was to create exquisite objects of art out of wood. I would watch fascinated as he sawed, planed, carved rough pieces of obstinate wood with his nicotine stained fingers and brought them to life. He used natural grains, colours, textures of a variety of wood to piece together salt and pepper cellars, toast racks, jewellery boxes, cigarette cases, ash trays. From a disc of a sapling with the bark intact he would create a myriad of useful, beautiful things.

Each article was perfectly fashioned in unusual shapes and designs of his imagination. Each object lovingly and ingeniously created was given away as a present. I got a doll made out of an acorn and reeds. Baba a cigarette case and ma a toast rack.

Apart from his carpentry what interested me most was his silver Rolex watch which he showed me often with not only date and month but it displayed phases of the moon every day. It didn't need any winding either. Marvellous!

His deft hands and imagination constantly at work produced delightful objects. He had certainly inherited his father's imagination but wrote his poems in wood.

Every holiday season loads of friends and relatives arrived at Chitrabhanu. Days were spent in joy and laughter but Rahtibabu never budged from his work table and Protima Devi from her morning room with intricate windows fitted with scores of little glass panes. She suffered from severe bouts of asthma.

The evenings were memorable. Guests and neighbours gathered in the spacious elegant drawing room for tea, music, Rabindranath's poems and songs selected by Protima Devi. Songs and music filled the air, reverberating through Chitrabhanu thrilling us as each guest took turns to sing or recite his everlasting compositions.

Through all this Rathibabu sat cross-legged on a special divan in his long robe. At seven in the evening a bowl of chicken soup arrived and set on a bed table in front of him. The rest of the delicately prepared light meal followed. His presence not his participation was enough at the soirees.

It was a great treat for me to be invited to Chitrabhanu for lunch. it was not only the delectable food but the ambiance and ritual that went with it. The smooth, polished, honey coloured dining table would be set with enormous silver *thalis* surrounded by six matching bowls, each containing delicious vegetable, fish and meat dishes all prepared according to Tagore family recipes.

After the sumptuous meal, came a little trolley to each guest, pushed by a bearer. It contained a wash basin with a tank underneath to catch the dirty water, well hidden from view and an antique copper jug of water for washing our hands. This ingenious little mobile hand washing trolley was devised by Rathibabu made out of contrasting red and white wood.

Scores of tourists come to see Chitrabhanu each year under the misconception that it belonged to Rabindranath Tagore. It was built long after his death. Protima Devi sold her beloved house to the West Bengal government who turned it into a Craft Training Centre for junior teachers.

Mr. And Mrs. Tagore passed away long ago but Chitrabhanu remains alive with their memories for me. When I walk through the house now I can hear the sound of laughter, poetry and Rabindra *Sangeet* reverberating not through the rafters but in a part of my brain where childhood memories are indelibly stored. I saw the rise and fall of Chitrabhanu. Hopefully, one day, this extraordinary, unique house our heritage, will be turned into a museum for everybody to admire and enjoy the legacy of a Master Craftsman.

Canine Capers

Every summer and *puja* holidays hordes of relatives and friends came to stay with the Tagores, next door, in Chitrabhanu and with us in Monjula. As there was plenty of water in Kalimpong in those days all guest were welcome.

Often Rathindranath Tagore's sister, Meera Devi came to spend summer with him and his wife, Pratima Devi. The crusty old lady with an ascorbic tongue was certainly not a favourite with us children. We always gave her a wide berth. This particular year even more so, as she had arrived with her two dearly beloved children. Two enormous alsatians dogs.

She was absolutely devoted to these creatures, they could do no wrong. She loved, pampered and spoilt them so much that they did what they pleased and paid scant heed to her commands.

Every morning she would brush their teeth with expensive toothpaste. She gave them their weekly bath in hot water liberally laced with eau de cologne and used imported dog soap. Their thick fur dried with fine Turkish towels. The ritual ended with a good dusting of lavender powder. Their beds too were cozy and comfortable with clean white sheets and pillows. To her disappointment they preferred to lie flat out, on their stomachs, on the cool cement floor instead.

Breakfast, lunch and dinner had to be served at precise times, on the polished honey hued dining table, before the humans partook of their meals. The dogs would sit on the dining chairs and lap up their food from their special bowls, laid on the table, supervised by their doting mother.

If one showed any reluctance to eat, she would coax and cajole him, pat his head and whisper words of encouragement and endearments in his furry ear. All doors and windows were tightly shut during their meal times so no one could disturb or distract them and spoil their delicate appetites. I would hide behind the wall and peep through the glass door to watch this ritual. Even ma didn't go to such lengths to feed me, a poor eater.

Right after their breakfast Meera Devi would take them out on their leashes for their morning constitution. They would stroll down Atisha Road leisurely, stopping and sniffing every bush to pee and poo, marking their territory. There were hardly any houses on Atisha Road those days and virtually no people on it, so it proved to be the ideal walking route for them.

One morning I was playing jack stones with the children staying in Chitrabhanu. We sat in the creeper covered stone gazebo which overlooked Atisha Road. From our vantage point, we had a clear view of the road as it went down and Meera Devi, as well, with her hounds going for their daily walk.

Suddenly one dog pricked up his ears and stood still. His eyes had focused on a slight movement in the bushes on the hillside far below. The other one was all attention too. They had spotted a poor goat, that must have strayed. He was munching grass merrily, oblivious of the danger that lurked above.

The two dogs reared, bounded up and charged simultaneously. Their leashes tightly strapped to Meera Devi's frail wrists, jerked her rudely out of her reverie as she went flying behind them. What took place next happened in minutes with devastating results.

We abandoned our game and clapped our hands in glee at the prospects of a fully fledged chariot race. A chariot race sans chariot, hounds instead of horses, leashes instead of reins, Atisha Road instead of the gorgeous Roman arena and just us children instead of the roaring Roman crowds! All the same, it smacked of excitement and we got our fill of it.

Meera Devi was no match for these two strong young dogs. She had no choice but to be dragged by them. Her top knot came loose, her salt and pepper straggly hair streamed behind her. One strap of her slipper snapped so the slipper got left behind. She limped along lopsided, her feet barely touching the ground. She opened her mouth to scream at the runaway team but a sudden bump on the road, sent her dentures flying out. They disappeared in the bushes. The *anchal* of her *saree* was fluttering and flying behind her; a white flag of peace. Her *saree*, was threatening to come off, eventually did!

The last few yards of this perilous journey she completed sliding down the hillside, off the road, in the most unlady like fashion, sitting on her bottom only in her blouse and petticoat.

"Stop! stop!" she cried red and furious. They did stop once they reached their goal, the poor unsuspecting goat. They had never seen a goat before so gingerly they started sniffing and inspecting it from all angles. Meera Devi now completely distraught undid their leashes with the most unholy epithets flowing out of her aristocratic mouth. All her terms of endearments for them forgotten.

The goat cornered, under careful scrutiny of these strange creatures, had no option but to defend himself and his right to graze, in the only way he could. Eyes dilated, wide with apprehension and fear, he reared on his hind legs, lowered his head, pointed his sharp sturdy horns at the fat rump of his nearest tormentor and charged with all his might.

The dog gave a yelp of surprise, put his woolly tail between his legs and made for home. The plucky little goat encouraged by his successful attack in getting rid of one enemy, was rearing up to demolish the next one. The dog completely bewildered by this turn of events decided to call it a day and followed his companion.

Meera Devi screamed at them to come back. They did not recognize the garbled commands coming out of her denture less mouth, even if they had, they wouldn't have paid any heed. They were not in the habit of obeying her.

Battered and bruised by thorny bushes, petticoat with large gashes, *saree*, retrieved and bundled under one arm, one forlorn slipper dangling from one hand, Meera Devi dragged herself home, exhausted. She looked as if she had been caught up in the most lethal and devastating of whirlwinds.

Rathibabu, Pratimadi and the guests were shocked to see her sorry state and cried out in unison, "What happened?" she was in no mood to answer.

The dogs had already arrived home and gone to sleep sprawled out on the verandah after their hectic excursion. They opened their eyes, gave her a cursory look and went back to sleep again.

Meera Devi usually joined us much later in the drawing room as she had to feed her dogs precisely at 7 p.m it also coincided with Rathibabu's dinner time. While the dogs ate in the tightly shut dining room, he ate sitting on his divan in the drawing room. He ate a very light meal of chicken soup, toast and boiled vegetables prepared by his personal cook. He cooked it and served it too, on a tray, placing it on a bed table on the divan.

One evening we were listening to Rabindra *sangeet* in the drawing room totally absorbed when loud terrified screams of "Save me, save me." greeted our ears from the dining room. I shot up, opened the connecting door to the dining room slightly and peeped in.

There was Maitrae Devi disheveled, running round the dining table with the two bounding dogs in hot pursuit barking loudly. Meera Devi stood aghast. She screamed at the dogs to stop but they were having too much fun to stop.

Maitrae Devi saw the chink in the door I had made, rushed at it, opening it wide, ran through and landed on Rathibabu's divan, upsetting the tray. The soup bowl jumped out of the tray and landed upside down on his lap.

The dogs were not far behind. Maitrae Devi was jumping up and down on the divan to keep her toes out of reach of the snarling, snapping jaws of the two vicious dogs. All eyes turned to look at this scene in disbelief. Mesmerized, everybody suddenly turned to stone.

Mrs. Roy kept holding her tea cup in midair, mouth open for a sip. The singer's mouth remained open too, though no sound came out. Mrs. Ghose sat immobile with a biscuit between her teeth. Mr. Das in the process of wiping his bald patch with his handkerchief sat with the handkerchief stuck on his head. Pratimadi sat with her asthma pump stuck to her nose. Ma, baba and others sat immobile. Meera Devi came rushing in screaming, not at the dogs but at the insensitive lady who was so inconsiderate as to disturb her precious babies at their meal. This she considered a personal affront.

Maitrae Devi was too hysterical to hear her. Her beautiful face a tomato red, eyes stark with terror, hair askew and *saree* threatening to part company.

It was Rathibabu who rose to the occasion and took control. He ordered Maitrae Devi to stop jumping, which now looked more and more like skipping. Very sternly, in a deep voice he addressed the frenzied dogs. "Sit down, sit down, sit down." they recognized the authority in his voice sat down reluctantly but mainly because their prey had stopping hopping. Still feet did not interest them. They were chained and led away by their mother grumbling about their ruined dinner.

Maitrae Devi sat down on the divan with a thump. Sweat pouring down her face, safe at last. Instantly, as if the play button had been pushed, people came alive. Mrs. Roy brought the tea cup to her lips at last; the songstress shut her gaping mouth but did not continue her song so rudely interrupted. Mrs. Ghose bit into her biscuit. Mr. Das brought his hanky down. Protima Devi pumped her rubber bulb vigorously once more.

All the petrified people in the room suddenly burst out into gales of laughter. The situation was too funny. They couldn't control themselves in spite of appearing rude to the injured party.

Maitrae Devi, the last of the guests, had arrived late that evening from Mungpoo. She had gone straight to her room to change and freshen up. Nobody had the chance to tell her about the rigid routine of the hounds in the house.

She had merrily barged into the dining room as usual to get to the adjoining drawing room when all hell broke loose. Taken by surprise she panicked and bolted. This was incentive enough for the dogs, bored with their dinner, to chase her hurtling figure and have some fun at her expense.

Meera Devi maintained that her precious darlings were merely boisterous puppies who loved to play and didn't mean any harm.

Todana

Todana is a Japanese style built-in cupboard with sliding doors. Baba had built these in both Monjulas as they are great space savers.

During *puja* usually in october, was the most delightful time for me. The bright, breezy, crisp days, just right for flying kites, eating guavas all afternoon from the garden, catching the fluttering techni-coloured butterflies and running up and down the green hillsides for the sheer joy of living. Ma did not object to any of my exuberant activities. She just let me run wild.

The house just below ours, Parboti, now Pine View, was rented out to a bumptious, reputed Hindi scholar who was compiling the most comprehensive Hindi to English dictionary in the solitude of Kalimpong.

Soon he became a regular tea time visitor at Monjula. He would sit with guests and ma on our large verandah sipping tea, enjoying the company and watching me play in the garden.

Another regular week end visitor was my cousin, Miss Bose. Unfortunately, she was my class teacher as well. A fat young lady well dressed. She applied layers and layers of make up on her face and reeked of the most expensive perfumes. She was jolly, friendly and people found her absolutely charming but no one knew what a tartar she was in the class room.

She seemed to derive great sadistic pleasure in terrorizing us. Her razor-sharp tongue always drew blood. To prove her impartiality to her cousin, poor me, she was harsher, ruder and stricter than to anyone else. My close friend were not spared either.

My best friend, Ganden, was a good student but being badgered constantly by Bosie, our nick name for her, she lost interest in her studies and started playing truant. I was a good student too, shy, quiet and obedient but constant faultfinding with never a word of praise or encouragement, was enough to kill my enthusiasm; since everything I did was never right, why bother. I became obstinate, bold and defiant.

One morning the sum that I had worked out was perfectly correct but finding no fault, she ordered me to rewrite it. I was furious. "I won't do it again," I retorted, surprised at myself. This was blatant disobedience and defiance. Something she was not used to. She flew into a violent rage, "Get out of my class and stay out," she ordered.

This was the first and last time I had been punished like this. Standing outside the class in the corridor was the most humiliating punishment that could be meted out. It meant standing in solitary confinement while teachers and children passed by giving knowing looks and smirks. The worst fear of all was the chance of Reverend Mother's appearance. This would give rise to an inquisition and punishment doubled.

I was not going to take such a risk. Being angry, hurt and humiliated, I took a far greater risk. I walked straight home, a most serious offence to walk out during school hours without permission.

Bosie's better sense prevailed due to love and affection for ma, I suppose, so she did not relate this incident to Reverend Mother but vehemently to ma instead. She threatened to go to Reverend Mother and dire consequences would follow if there was a repetition. Ma was shocked and horrified at her beloved, docile child's behaviour. I was subjected to a good tongue lashing as a result.

How does one hit back at a tyrant? The first step was easiest of all. I poured out half the bottle of her expensive perfume down the drain and refilled it with water, to the exact level again, during one of her visits to Monjula. She sensed it and complained to ma. Another tongue lashing from ma followed but there was no proof. The second step was even simpler. I asked the cook to put a good amount of *chili* powder in her soup every time until she would shiver and shake at the very sight of soup.

She always wore beautiful georgette *sarees*, to appear slim. I had been brought up to the first row of seats from the third row in the class, so that she could keep an eye on me. Now, I was directly behind her as she wrote on the blackboard. I took my pen, pointed it at her broad back and shook it vigorously. The ink spurted out in a spray as precisely as a water pump, used during *holi*. The whole class watched in shocked silence as tiny dots of black ink, covered the pastel *anchal*.

I was well satisfied with my efforts. Class was over, she was leaving the room. Everyone gasped. Those little ink dots had spread out into huge, big monstrous patches. I was doomed. Fortunately she did not connect the discoloration of her pretty *saree* to an act of sabotage.

Bosie wore *choli*s with deeply cut necklines. I had collected three vicious, large, black ants in my geometry box. Their bites caused excruciating pain. every afternoon we had to go, four at a time, to her desk to get our exercise books corrected. This was my chance. I stood directly behind her as the others crowed around her, well aware of my plan.

I opened the geometry box, using the divider as pincers; I picked up an ant to drop it on her wide bare back. It wriggled free and landed on her *anchal.* Second one landed on the folds of her *saree,* the third one on her chair. All three ant bombs were mishits. I had run out of ammunition. I was disappointed. The ants were fast; they scampered down and ran on the floor looking for a bolt hole for safety!

All this time the girls were watching operation ants with bated breath. Once the ants started running all over the floor, all hell broke loose. "Ants! Ants!" they cried terrified as if a box of snakes had been let loose instead of three mere little ants. Books, pens, pencils, rulers went flying as they climbed on their desks, screaming at the top of their voices.

Bosie was taken aback by this sudden uproar. "Shut up and sit down," she roared. She was proud of the fact that she had the quietest and most manageable class in the whole school. The girls were having the time of their lives; they were not going to be shouted down. They were playing their parts well. They demonstrated a perfect rendition of mass hysteria.

Months of curbed emotions and frustration now spilled over. They shouted, screamed, yelled and jumped to their heart's content.

Bosie shook like jelly, red in the face, arms raised, clenched fists while rivulets of sweat flowed down her face making deep trenches through her heavy makeup. Her neat *khopa* flew open dislodging the false hair inside. "Stop it! Stop it!" she screamed as missiles flew around barely missing her!

The door flew open, the next door teacher had come to find out what the pandemonium was all about. She was aghast to find the girls gone berserk and Bosie a human atom bomb about to explode and send up the biggest mushroom cloud ever.

She took the heavy wooden blackboard duster and rapped it hard on a desk. "Now stop it!" she said sternly. We stopped dead. We had our fun. This was far better than any sting the poor ants could have delivered. "Now, tell me what is the matter girls?" the teacher demanded. "Ants miss, ants," somebody whispered. "Where?" "Right there," she said pointing to the helpless little ants on the floor, still running around madly looking for shelter.

Bosie stared at the little creatures in disbelief. Her flushed, contorted face relaxed. She collapsed on her chair in a heap, covered her sweaty face with her fat hands. We watched her in suspenseful silence. Was she having a heart attack?

Her whole body started shaking slowly, then faster and faster, the rolls of fat between her *choli* and *saree,* rippled like the bellows of a concertina. Suddenly she flung back her head and burst out laughing. She roared with uncontrollable laughter until tears rolled down her face. We were completely taken aback. This was not the reaction we had expected. Well, if we had failed to give her a heart attack, at least, we had managed to drive her stark raving mad.

Next morning she appeared in class, much to our disappointment, perfectly made up, in full control of her senses.

For the rest of the girls the harassment ended once class was over but for me there was no respite, it carried on as she visited Monjula every week end. Ma was always sweet, gently and kind, never uttered a harsh word to me but every time Bosie came over she had tons of complaints against me. She told ma that I was not to be friendly with Ganden, she was a bad influence on me. Ma in turn, would give me a severe tongue lashing after Bosie's visits which left me furious.

Ganden and I are still the best of friends. Bosie had failed to part us. If only she could have seen Ganden in later years when she always came first in class and nothing less.

Durga puja was on. I had holidays but I was made to study for hours as Bosie kept reminding ma of the impending final exams. and that I would surely fail unless, I studied hard. To add fuel to the fire the supercilious old man, the Hindi scholar, told ma very seriously that her daughter, playing around with the *chokras* was unbecoming, unladylike and wild with no signs of serious attention to studies. She would have to take steps to control me or I would become a complete ruffian.

Ma was shocked and worried. Nobody had ever criticized her beloved little daughter. Now this eminent scholar plus my class teacher were predicting dire consequences if she did not take steps to control my boundless energy and channel it into monstrous, laborious methods to gain knowledge.

That morning I had been sitting at my study table for hours listening to my friends playing outside. Out of sheer boredom I started decapitating the flowers from the vase. I took a pithy stem and wrote "I hate Bosie" on the white wall. The watery sap made no imprint at all.

I was about to leave the room as my study time was nearly over when ma sauntered in. "Where are you going?" she asked sternly. "I have finished revising." "But your two hours are not up yet, you..." she didn't finish her sentence. She was staring at the wall behind me. "What is this?" she asked horrified pointing at the wall. I turned around and there in huge bold green letters was "I hate Bosie" staring at me more prominent than any neon sign.

The sap had interacted with the lime on the wall, dried and appeared clearly. "How can you write such things about people?" she thundered. "I am thoroughly ashamed of your behaviour. You are supposed to be studying and not writing posters on the wall. You have done so poorly in all your tests. You will surely fail the finals." "I don't care if I fail." "What, you don't care?," with that she landed a slap on my face. I was stunned. I couldn't believe it. Ma slapping me. She had never ever done that. I was mortally wounded.

The slap did not hurt me; it was too weak to kill a fly. I was hurt, hurt inside. Tears of anger and sorrow welled up in my eyes. I fled blindly out of her presence and out of the house. I had no idea where I was going. I ran down the steps to the outhouse and locked myself in one of the dark empty *godowns.* I lay on the cold, damp, cement floor sobbing my heart out.

Sometime later, I heard footsteps passing my door and *kanchi's,* voice calling out my name. Then nothing. Hours passed. I had no idea what time it was as no light penetrated my dark dungeon. Nobody was looking for me. That was strange. No commotion, no search parties, nothing, only silence. Ma didn't care for me; she did not love me that's why she wasn't looking for me. In that case I wasn't going back.

Eventually hunger, cold and darkness overpowered my determination. I opened the door. It was pitch dark. I made my way up to the main house. I stood at the open back door watching the cook calmly, cooking dinner. As soon as his head was turned I slipped into the house, ran up the stairs noiselessly in my bare feet. Lights were blazing in every room but the house was empty. Only *Kanchi* was ironing in the bedroom.

No ma, she must have gone to see the *puja,* in town. I waited for *Kanchi* to leave the room. The minute she got out, I got in through another door. The sliding door of the *todana* was open. I quickly climbed up the shelves to the top most wide compartment where quilts were stored. It was large enough to hold my full length. I pulled the sliding door shut and dozed off.

Suddenly I heard a voice and peeped through a crack in the door. Ma was in the arms of Maitrae Devi in a state of collapse. She was gasping for breath, her voice a hoarse whisper, repeating my name over and over again. She was desperately sliding the doors of the *todana,* down below to see if I was hiding there. She never thought of looking for me just above.

Maitrae Devi was trying to comfort and soothe a distraught and disheveled ma. She kept giving water to wet her parched lips and throat, dry with fear. They looked under the beds, every nook and corner, made their way down and out of the house.

My heart broke at the havoc I had caused to ma's mental and physical state. After all it was not her fault; she still loved me and wanted me back. It was the work of those two devilish, arrogant, know all pundits who had poisoned her mind against me. Where were they now, were they looking for me or giving ma any support in her distress? My heart went out to her but I was not going to give in, I had to be found. But how, they would never look for me up here.

I slid my door half way but *Kanchi,* was still busy ironing and didn't look up. Desperately wanting to be discovered, I stuck one foot out, left it dangling for *Kanchi,* to see. Eventually, she did, gave a gasp and tugged at it. I pretend to be fast asleep. Ma returned and grabbed me to her heart sobbing with relief. I held her tight and swore never to put her through this agony ever again. She forgave me but everybody thought I needed a good spanking.

The enormity and extent of the search for the lost girl was brought home to me by ma's accusing friends next day.

While I lay holed up in the dark dungeon, the whole area around Monjula and Atisha Road had been searched with a fine toothed comb. Ma had sent emissaries to Bahadur's house. He made matters worse by stating that, I was in the habit of gathering special leaves, on a particular steep cliff, for my guinea pigs. Perhaps I had slipped, fallen and broken my neck. There was no sign of me dead or alive.

Ma then formed a search party and went to town to look for me. Just about everybody was in the *Durga Puja pandal,* watching a play. Ma was only interested to meet Dr. Boral. A good friend and a very influential man. He was not available as he was acting on the stage. Not daunted, ma got the ushers to bring down the curtain and stop the play. This was an emergency after all.

Dr. Boral came out unrecognizable in his stage make up. She begged him to send out a red alert and to announce over the mike. if anyone had seen me. In the police station, reluctantly, the police swung into action and rang up the police out post at Teesta Bazar with my description.

Then she went to St. Joseph Convent to look for me. The holy nuns were at their evening prayers. Ma managed to pry Reverend Mother Philip from the church to ask her if I was in the convent. Reverend Mother was not perturbed by this news of my disappearance. She said she would pray for my safe return and went back to her prayers.

Everybody in Kalimpong was looking for me. I was the perpetrator of the biggest child hunt in the history of Kalimpong!

Birthday Parties

My birthday parties, thrown by my parents every year in Kalimpong, are remembered to this day by those who attended them, even by those who didn't. Most of my school friends are now spread out all over the world and when I meet them, they enthusiastically reminiscence about those parties and the great times we shared. I also meet old students from my school, St. Joseph's Convent who never attended my parties, yet remember them in great detail.

"How is it that you remember my parties so well when you never attended them?" I ask surprised. "We were not invited but used to hear about them from those who were and we were plain jealous." My friends remember me on my birthday every year as it falls on a very important day when India celebrates its Independence Day 15th August.

My parents loved to entertain and birthday parties were always special. Baba arrived from Calcutta loaded with goodies. Streamers, balloons, miniature national flags and return gifts. All dignitaries, friends, along with their children, my whole class, class teacher and nuns were invited for the birthday bash.

In the lower classes there were a few boys in my class but they were never invited as there was strict segregation of sexes in those days. The nuns too were reluctant to come as they were forbidden to attend parties, however, innocent. They usually came two at a time, their veils lowered to cover their faces as much as possible.

Two little Anglo-Indian girls with blue eyes and long blond hair, Felicity & Fleur, were strictly forbidden by their parents, to attend any parties, specially, I suppose, at a native's residence. Two girls, Elizabeth and Irene, daughters of the Convent, were always invited along with my young friend Betty Dutt, whose birthday happened to fall on the same day as mine.

Baba spent the whole day decorating the long dining room with streamers and balloons, while ma got busy setting the two tables for Betty and me. She had to supervise the mounds of food that had to be cooked at home. As there was no bakery, Bahadur, our cook, would spend the previous day painstakingly baking two cakes for Betty and me. He would spend hours beating the batter, then bake the cakes in a make shift oven, made out of a kerosene tin, over a charcoal fire. The whole house soon filled with the aroma of the baking cakes.

The party fare was always the same. Simple but substantial and absolutely delicious. Rich mutton curry, made out of solid chunks of meat, *cholar dal* with fried coconut pieces. Round white *luchies,* puffed to perfection. Mango chutney, creamy white *payesh* and ma's famous conch shaped *Sandesh* that melted in the mouth, cups of steaming hot tea and last of all the birthday cake circled by candles. This meal was looked forward to with great anticipation by my class friends who were all boarders, subjected to the insipid food at the Convent. They certainly did justice to the food.

The girls ate in silence, savouring and relishing each morsel until I would break their concentration by playing word games or whispering games which always come out distorted through mouthful of food, sending us into gales of laughter. We enjoyed and thrived on such simple pleasures. The cakes were cut to loud strains of Happy Birthday and polished off with great relish.

Once high tea was over, we spilled out on the lawn to play various games. Treasure Hunt being most popular. Then I had the brilliant idea of having a fancy dress. There were *almirahs* full off old clothes collected by my parents from all over the world. They were out dated and never used but were too good to be discarded.

I crammed a tea chest with all the clothes I could find. In another box I stored the props, walking sticks, spectacles, umbrellas, fans, hand bags, shoes, hats and costume jewellery. A table contained powder, rouge, lipstick, eye brow pencil and paint.

The girls got busy mixing and matching the clothes, using necessary props to go with their outfits. After much giggling, shouting, screaming and grabbing, they were ready with exaggerated make up, to parade in front of my parents and their guests vying for the prize declared by ma for the most innovative costume.

Ma clapped her hands in glee marveling at the transformation of the school girls into poised, lords, ladies, Maharajas, Maharanis to dainty, coy Japanese ladies, to menacing pirates and bandits. Ma could not decide on the best costume. "They are all so good, all of them deserve a prize!" she exclaimed. The fancy dress competitions were hilarious, always a great success and great fun.

As we grew older childish games gave way to dancing parties. We waltzed and fox-trotted to Victor Sylvester's orchestra, Frank Sinatra and Bing Crosby's songs played on the hand cranked gramophone, operated by Easther Cohen who was not interested in such frivolous pastime as dancing.

The male sex was sorely missed on these occasions but where to find them and how to invite them were major problems.

When the party ended the nuns gathered up the gaggle of girls who were reluctant to go back to the dreary confines of the Convent. Loaded with sweets, chocolates, balloons, they would run down the steep *chorbato* waving the tiny Indian flags.

Once back in the Convent they would be besieged by the whole school to give them a detailed account of the party as if it was Cinderella's ball that they had missed. The party goers of course regaled them with minute details making them green with envy.

One year my party turned out to be a disaster. All invitations were given and accepted. Dressed in my party frock I waited for my class friends to arrive. There was no sign of them. Minutes turned into an hour. All other guests had arrived. The nuns were always very punctual, so why this delay? Eventually the Superior, Mother Marie Joseph, Mother John Mary and Irene arrived minus the girls. The nuns apologized profusely for the absence of the girls.

They had insisted on going up to the Homes to see a film, Henry V instead of coming to my party. I was devastated. I couldn't believe my ears. My friends who always looked forward to my parties had opted to see a film instead. They had defied the nuns, something unheard of. I held back the tears of disappointment and anger that threatened to spill out and make furrows down my powdered cheeks.

I sat through the party glum and bleary eyed, smarting from the pain of rejection. It was the most miserable party I ever had. I moped around, listless and unhappy with my two day scholar friends. Suddenly Attay, the deaf and dumb, handy man of the convent arrived breathlessly with a letter for Mother Superior.

All colour drained off her face as she read the note. "I must go back to the Convent at once, one of the buses carrying the girls up to the Homes, has met with an accident," she cried. Shock waves ran through my whole body, my dear friends hurt perhaps dead.

My pent up tears flowed unabated, not of anger or disappointment but anxiety. Everybody had been shocked to silence. "What terrible news," wept ma. "Hope nobody is badly hurt," breathed baba. I was too stunned for words. "Please God, let my friends be safe," I prayed fervently. The party came to an abrupt end.

There were no telephones so there was no news of knowing exactly what happened until I reached school next morning. The nuns usually walked the girls up to the Homes in crocodile formation but this time Mr. Tashi Tshering, a transport operator and a good friend of the school, had ery generously offered two of his buses to take the girls up to the Homes. This was an added attraction apart from the film. The girls, teachers and nuns had happily piled into the buses. This was going to save them a five mile hike up the steep mountain slope.

The first bus had groaned its way up the winding road easily. The second bus, way behind, was unable to manoeuvre a sharp bend, went off the road, rolled over twice and came to a halt upside down on a rice field.

Miraculously the girls escaped with just a few cuts and bruises but were in a state of shock. Mother Cecelia had passed out with a bump on her head. During this time she found herself in heaven only to wake up to the disappointing reality at finding herself back on earth again.

When I entered my classroom that morning, I found the girls relating their harrowing experience animatedly, to those who were not in the bus, displaying cuts and bruises proudly. They were the heroines of the day. The minute they spotted me at the door, everybody fell silent and buried their heads in their books. There was pin drop silence.

They couldn't face me. They had refused to come to my party and gone to see a movie instead. In the process, a bus load of girls had almost been killed. Was it divine providence? The girls never missed my birthday parties ever again!

An Unusual Nun

The very first time I set my eyes on a nun, I was terrified. Enveloped in a billowing black and blue attire, a white face framed in a white window. The white hands seemed to have a life of their own, without being attached to this big bundle in any way. She must be a *bokshi I* decided, mentioned by Bahadur, so often, in his ghost stories. I was well aware about their diabolic, devilish devices. Frightened, I hid behind ma's back and peeped at this apparition anxiously, with growing concern.

This apparition happened to be Mother Philip, the Superior of St. Joseph's Convent in Kalimpong. Ma had taken me down to the Convent for admission.

Once back home, I ran to find Bahadur to tell him that I had seen a *bokshi* at last. Surprisingly, she had been kind and gentle, not like the ones depicted in his frightening stories that cast spells on innocent people and relished eating little children. Bahadur laughed out loud, "You stupid girl. The one you met today is not a *bokshi,* in fact just the opposite, a holy person, a nun." Funny, that the nun should be dressed in black like a *bokshi* I thought.

When I eventually joined school, my teacher in K.G. Was a short little nun, Mother Cecelia. We called her Mother although she was neither married nor had children. The little bundle had frank light blue eyes. A mere stern glance from those eyes would bring silence and order in the class in a thrice. Yet these very eyes would light up with merriment at the slightest hint of a joke.

Since we could not depend on her body language for a cue, body being entangled in a shapeless black tent, from head to toe, we read her face or what little of it showed in the white frame. Her eyes gave away her moods. Apart from her eyes, her great, booming voice did the rest. A bark from her and we would be quaking in our shoes. I could never fathom how this little bundle, generated such a powerful voice which could be heard clearly from one end of our enormous play ground, to the other.

I don't think Mother Cecelia had any formal training in teaching. In those days nuns were only trained to be nuns. Mother happened to be a born teacher. Her teaching methods very simple but effective, she made learning fun. Every morning we started by reciting our tables from 2 to 12 in a sing song fashion. We enjoyed this, learnt them effortlessly and remember them to this day.

Lessons were never too long or boring. She would find some amusing diversion to relax our little brains. She was definitely fonder of bold, naughty, lively children. Her favourite was bold, brassy, plump Bridget Dobbin. Not very interested in her lessons, she would constantly find ways and means to distract Mother.

She always sat on the first row, just under Mother's large nose. Bridget would suddenly remember some pressing incident past or present, interrupt Mother to relate it vigorously, loudly with much action. Mother's blue eyes would dance with merriment, regardless of how insignificant or nonsensical the story. This always proved to be a welcome break and we would all join in the fun and laughter. Mother's unrestricted, open hearted laughter was as loud as her voice and very infectious.

Mother had several favourites. Amongst those was a very handsome, cherubic boy with green eyes and silky brown hair called Carl. He did not meet Mother's standard of a live wire, boisterous child but his beautiful big green eyes and angelic face made everyone fall in love with him.

Bridget basked in Mother's leniency and bullied us whole sale. We hated her elevated position and her bullying tactics so we were elated when she overstepped her mark one day. Mother picked up the long, thin flexible stick which lay on her desk and whipped her fat bottom soundly. Bridget let out few sharp, surprised shrieks and couldn't sit down for quite a few days.

Bridget the dancing, prancing, boisterous, carefree girl with the attention span of a cricket, talked, laughed and joked, we on the other hand didn't dare open our mouths. I was totally tongue tied, mortified even to ask permission to visit the toilet. This led to disaster of course. Mother didn't say a word when she noticed the puddle under my chair. She just gave me a withering look. That was bad enough but worst was the jeers of my class mates for days.

Mother taught the K.G. Class for years and years, guiding hundreds of children through the whole series of Radiant Readers. All the children of the Raja Dorji family passed through her capable hands. Her Royal Highness Kesang Dorji the Queen Mother of Bhutan never forgot her. She sent Mother a 40 pound cake from Flurys Calcutta for her golden Jubilee. She was invited to the young King's coronation in Bhutan.

The children she taught are spread out all over the world today. They all remember her with deep affection. She made a large impact on all of us, not only because she was the first teacher we encountered, in our young impressionable lives but she was such a dynamic person.

I couldn't think of anyone more deserving than mother when she received the President's gold medal for the best teacher of the year. But she never got the post of a superior.

Mother was a bundle of activity with phenomenal energy. She was the driving force behind every function that took place in our school. With her powerful voice she would lead the choir. Organize every concert to perfection, teaching us to dance, sing and act out short plays. She taught us square dancing. She was a good dancer and loved to dance, sing and coach us for all the games we played. She would be running up and down, blowing her whistle and shouting out orders and strategies while teaching us to play hockey.

She took us to picnics to distant places, Rinkingpong, Delo, Relli and Teesta. Hitching up her voluminous habit, she would nimbly maneuver, on her short legs, all the steep precarious *chorbatos* to these distant spots.

She was everywhere, guiding, teaching and accompanying us with great enthusiasm. There was nothing she wouldn't try her hand at and couldn't do. Her sheer joy of living, vivacity and eagerness fired our imagination and encouraged us to perform better with great enjoyment. She was fun to be with. She turned everything into an enjoyable adventure.

Mother always accompanied the children to Dr. Graham's Homes to see an English movie. This trek was done on foot but that particular year, two big buses had been hired to take the girls up. Mother was in the second bus with her wards while the first bus sped on ahead. Unfortunately the brakes of her bus failed. The driver couldn't take the steep turn and the bus rolled down the mountain side.

My birthday party was in full swing when news arrived that the bus carrying my friends had met with a terrible accident. The mood of the whole party turned from jollity to gloom.

In spite of the bus tumbling down hill, no major catastrophe occurred. The children and Mother Cecelia in the bus had been bumped, thumped and rolled over and over. Shoes and skirts flew. Mother's petticoat and voluminous layers of garments flew around in the most inappropriate, shameful and outrageous manner until the bus came to a halt at last. A few of the girls had received minor injuries but Mother had been knocked out cold for several minutes.

When I met Mother this is the story of the accident she related to me. "My eyes were shut. I knew I was in heaven. I was blissfully happy, getting ready to meet St. Peter at the gate. I opened my eyes to look at him; instead, I saw branches of trees and green grass. How much like our good old earth heaven is I thought. Then I saw the girl's anxious faces peering at me and realized I was still on good old earth. What a disappointment!"

For days all that was visible were black and blue marks on Mother's white face, her whole body too must have been black and blue from the severe battering received in the bus, giving rise to great pain. She cheerfully attended class as usual. Nothing could keep her in bed till the very last years of her life.

Tripping off to see a classical English movie at the Homes was rare but Mother took the girls frequently to see exciting cowboy movies and smash hits from Hollywood to Novelty, the only cinema hall in Kalimpong. It was constructed entirely of corrugated tin sheets so the girls named it the Tin Pot

Palace. It contained wooden benches crawling with bed bugs. The mosquitoes too joined them gleefully for a voracious meal of the Convent girls.

She took the crocodile of girls for a long walk every Sunday but much more exciting for Mother and the girls was to witness a football match at the *Mela* ground. Mother, along with the girls, always came back hoarse after cheering the home team lustily.

Mother enjoyed everything, specially eating. She had a sweet tooth. She loved ice creams so did we all but no such delicacy was available in Kalimpong in those fridge-less days. Mother had accompanied us to Darjeeling, to St. Joseph's School for a hockey match. We were given a sumptuous lunch followed by several big bowls of ice-cream. I was sitting beside Mother. Between the two us we polished off one bowl. She was like a small child enjoying her first ice-cream. Her blue eyes sparkled as she scraped the bowl, smacking her lips and licking the spoon in the most unladylike fashion!

Mother loved to eat and that is what gave her all that extra energy and vitality. She never walked demurely like the other nuns. She ran. High spirited and energetic she never seemed to tire. Each day, was an adventure for her. She enjoyed life to the full in the close confines of the convent walls and her cumbersome habit.

She charmed everyone she came in contact with, parents, visitors, royalty. She put them at ease immediately with her hearty laughter and winning ways. They just adored her and came back to see her again and again, long after their wards had left the school.

The past pupils came from all over the world to meet her specially. She remembered each one, their names and their special attributes. She was not soft spoken, gentle, piously demure like the other nuns. She exuded lethal doses of charm and sparkling vivacity which no one could resist.

She was all in all in the convent and the whole school revolved around her. The Convent was her only home. In 1936, St. Joseph's Convent was taking shape when she arrived as a young nun from far away Scotland. She spent the rest of her life here except for a short stint in Bethany School, Darjeeling. She devoted and dedicated her whole life not only to teaching but educating children to grow to their full potential and bloom.

Unfortunately her strong, sturdy legs which had given her so much service, packed up. The last few years of her life she was unable to walk. This was a great blow to her. She was forced to retire from her high spirited life. The Queen Mother of Bhutan, learning of her condition, sent her a wheel chair immediately. Now she was confined in her small room and the long wooden passage.

Her brain worked perfectly and so did her robust heart which refused to stop. She insisted on eating eggs and sausages for breakfast every day. She would throw tantrums if there were no sausages on any day. Both these items persistently banned by the doctors. "Bad for the heart," they said but these didn't have the slightest ill effect on her vigorous heart.

I went to visit her one morning. She was sitting at her table, looking out of the window day dreaming. No invalid's dress for her. She was fully attired in the ample folds of her usual nun's clothing. Her sharp blue eyes looked faded and the twinkle had been replaced by a seriousness I had never seen before. The most salient feature her joyous, free flowing laughter that rose, straight from her heart and spilled out loud and clear, was woefully missing.

She kept going back to her childhood and her beloved Scotland.

She was very upset as she had lost her brother recently. "I am the last one left now" she sighed.

Slowly she sank into deep slumber, sleeping day and night. All the verve and vitality had gone out of her bouncing body but her strong heart kept beating till the age of 84 until she slipped away peacefully in her sleep.

She lived her life to the brim, giving us so much of herself. Teaching us how to live and enjoy life now she lives in our hearts forever.

Achar Bottles, Dearer than Life

Ma called her Sobhadidi and so did I. I should have addressed her as *Mashi* as I did all ma's close friends. Somehow, I felt that this cold and frosty lady was far from close to my sweet, gentle mother. I couldn't get myself to address her as *'Mashi'* even for propriety's sake.

The first time ma and I met Sobhadi, she was lying in bed with some imaginary disease. Her white oval face was white as the sheet she was laying on, her curly black hair controlled by a tight knot. She barely acknowledged ma and me when her husband introduced us. Her colourless lips remained shut in a straight thin line.

Ma, feeling sorry for this poor woman confined to her bed, started to show concern and sympathy for her. She responded by turning on her side and presenting her back to us. We got the message loud and clear, she did not want company, sympathy, polite, conversation and certainly no invasion of her privacy.

This was the first time we were invited by my doctor to go upstairs to meet his wife although; we were frequent visitors to his chamber. There was no reason for us to go into the house as I was only a patient, accompanied by ma, waiting, like all the others to be treated professionally and not sociably. Usually we sat in the visiting room teeming full of patients until called into the doctor's chamber for consultation.

Actually, there was nothing wrong with me. It was ma who was the hypochondriac where I was concerned. At the slightest hint of a cold, a single sneeze, I would be hauled off, not to our family doctor but to the most famous and best pediatrician of Calcutta at that time. Dr. Gopal Banerjee.

Ma had lost my sister Monjula, not too long ago and she lived in a state of perpetual terror of losing me. Doctor Banerjee soon realized that I was perfectly healthy and required no medication. To please ma, he prescribed tonics the worst tasting one being Ferradol.

He also discovered that ma was a very progressive and well informed lady with great ideas about improving the lot of down trodden and helpless women. He took to discussing various interesting topics with her for hours, while the line of patients in the waiting room lengthened and spilled out into the street as I sat quietly like a good child, bored to tears.

I would start fidgeting and gently hint about going home after my long stint in a straight jacket.

Ma would make a move to go feeling guilty about the dozens of patients waiting outside. He could easily have attended to half a dozen patients during the time we spent with him. He would allay ma's guilty feeling and persuade her to stay little longer. To persuade me was more difficult, so to reduce my boredom, to carry on his animated conversation with ma, he would keep me entertained with books and stories. Then, one day, he discovered my interest in firearms and knives and his eyes lit up as he loved firearms too.

All adults but not the doctor frowned at my fascination for guns. They predicted dire consequences. Phulan Devi did not exist then yet, they predicted a similar future for me, or worse. They found it so unusual for a little girl to be interested in lethal weapons instead of playing with pretty lifeless dolls.

The visit upstairs to the doctor's bedroom that day was to show me his collection of guns. Unfortunately, his ailing wife occupied that room most of the time. She obviously did not like visitors, especially not patients. They were faceless, nameless individuals who had no business to go beyond her husband's chamber, invade her privacy and her only sanctuary, the bedroom. They were a necessary evil who took up so much of her husband's time and energy. Not that she hankered for his company but at least, she got his ear to unleash volleys from her ever acidic tongue, pickled in vinegar!

The doctor unperturbed by his wife's uncouth behaviour, being used to it, opened a steel cupboard which contained several guns of different sizes. I gaped at this treasure trove open mouthed. I handled each gun but couldn't lift most of the heavy ones. Then, to my utter surprise, he produced the smallest, most perfect hand gun; I had ever laid eyes on. I took it from his proffered hand gently, almost reverently. It was light as a feather and fitted into my small hand snugly. I fell in love with it instantly, respect and admiration for the good doctor went up in my estimation.

Although, we went up to meet the doctor's wife, Sobha, a few times, ma couldn't penetrate her frostiness. We would find her standing on the verandah wrapped in a white *saree* with a narrow border, enhancing her coldness.

Straight, thin and tall, much taller than the doctor, she looked like a ghost to me. Ma charmed people easily. They fell prey to her simplicity, sincerity and joyful laughter but not Sobhadi. Ma was not able to break through Sobhadi's impregnable, icy fortress.

The doctor soon became a firm family friend. A man of boundless energy, sheer vitality, good humour and fun. He was the very antithesis of his wife. An icicle, swathed in a white *saree*, the imagery was real.

We were unpleasantly and the doctor pleasantly surprised when his wife, condescended to accompany him for a short holiday to Kalimpong at Monjula. It was not because she was eager to accompany her husband and generously bestow the pleasure of her company on him but for her own selfish reasons. A holiday in the hills during the midst of summer would surely revive her delicate imagined, disease ridden body, she calculated.

Ma was most apprehensive about her coming to stay with us but baba was unperturbed. Monjula was full of guests with their children when the doctor and his wife arrived. The guests took to the doctor immediately. He entertained them amply with anecdotes and jokes sending them into gales of laughter. Sobhadi would sit knitting quietly not amused in the least and speak only, to contradict him.

She always refused to accompany the gang of guests with their enthusiastic leader, the doctor, for sightseeing, walks, singing sessions on the lawn. Ma kind and thoughtful kept her company while the others went out. Ma not only missed out on all the fun but was forced to listen to all the uncharitable comments Sobhadi passed on every single guest and their children in their absence.

Ma, who always overlooked people's faults and short comings was appalled by her narrow minded remarks and defended them stoutly, only to be told that she was blind and stupid, totally incapable of judging characters. Eventually, ma, instead of listening to her malicious remarks about her friends and relatives, took to busying herself with household chores to avoid her.

Nothing ever pleased Sobhadi. She found fault with everything and everybody, especially us children. We were neither to be seen nor heard. She not only admonished us severely if we made the slightest noise but our parents as well, for their lack of upbringing. In her sharp, piercing eyes, we were a bunch of ill-mannered hooligans bound to grow up into murderers, bandits and *goondas*. We had no choice but to swallow her insults. We in turn stuck out our tongues and made faces at her, behind her back. I tried it once, facing her, with dire consequences.

At table, whenever people enjoyed a certain dish and praised the cook, she would declare in her sweetest tone, "How could you eat it, there is no salt in it." There would be pin drop silence all around. The food was always too rich, too hot, not sweet enough or downright inedible.

At last they left and everybody heaved a deep sigh of relief. We missed the doctor whose exuberance and high spirits had kept the group in a state of great excitement and activity.

Next summer brought dismal news. Doctor was going abroad, so Sobhadi had decided to visit Monjula again but mercifully, not as our guest but as a tenant. She wanted to be alone, have complete peace and quiet so she demanded, rather than ask, for our small flat in the annex. Ma readily agreed but refused to take any rent. After all, the good doctor had not charged ma a penny for the umpteen consultations.

Sobhadi arrived with bag and baggage minus servant. Ma was dismayed, how could she possibly manage, she wondered. She soon found out how. This visit of hers where she wanted to be self sufficient and absolutely on her own turned out to be just the opposite.

Every morning she would come and sit on our verandah with her knitting. She would spend most of the morning there. She would appear again at tea time to have hot cups of tea and snacks. As night fell, she would make herself comfortable in the drawing room to everyone's discomfort. Her very presence was enough to dry up all conversation. Her constant proximity to us was certainly not in keeping with her resolution of being on her own.

She did her own cooking but made our *Kanchi* do all the washing up. As she cooked she would come asking for a spoonful of turmeric or *jeera* or *garam masala* and almost everything she required, did not have at hand and made no effort to buy.

She never went to the market but always gave ma a list of things she wanted. Her list consisted of five potatoes, three onions, five *potols,* two tomatoes, two *brinjals,* one lemon etc., all according to numbers and not by weight. Each vegetables had to be of a certain size and absolutely fresh or all hell would break loose.

Ma found it impossible to buy vegetables according to numbers. Eventually she started giving vegetable from her own shopping bag. Ma harassed by her constant demands wished she had rather stayed with us. It would have been much simpler.

Every summer, ma made bottles of delicious, mouth watering *achar* with green mangoes. She always made a very large quantity as most of it got pilfered by me and my friends, long before they matured in the hot sun.

Shobadi watched ma making mango *achar* with great interest. She calculated that if she made her own *achar* she would not have to buy tasteless ones at an exorbitant price from the market. If she made enough it would last her through the whole year. It would be a great saving indeed. She didn't need to save at all, her husband had pots of money but she was too tight fisted to spend any of it.

She was now determined to make mango *achar*. Of course it fell on ma's shoulder again to select perfect green mangoes, buy them and slice them as Sobhadi did not have a *bothi* for that purpose. Surely she could have borrowed ours as everything else and sliced the mangoes herself.

Moreover I couldn't figure out why she was making sour *achar* when she was sour enough! Surely she was not pregnant! *Kanchi* did all the grinding of *masalas*. She put in more effort into hours of grinding in the hope of a handsome *baksish* which never came her way.

All that Sobhadi did was to mix the *masala* with the mango slices, add oil and bottle them with loving care. Ma had to provide bottles too, a rare commodity in those days. Sobhadi guarded the bottle with her life.

She spent sleepless afternoons guarding the bottles, in neat rows, as they dried on her roof top. She was not taking any chances. She was sure we hooligans would dip our dirty little fingers into her precious bottles and finish them. Our little fingers itched to do just that, more out of spite than greed. All our efforts of emptying the bottles were of no avail. She was always around, her sharp eyes focused on those bottles!

At last the blessed day for her departure arrived. Ma reserved a seat for her in Rambabu's station wagon, with a wooden body. It was one of the few taxis plying between Kalimpong and Siliguri in those days. She was seated in the taxi, while her baggage went on the carrier on top along with her precious *achar* bottles, carefully packed in a large basket.

We children were delighted to see her depart. No more talking in hushed tones, tip-toeing around the house to spare her extra sharp ears, as sharp as her tongue, from noise. No more lectures, tongue lashing, stony disapproving stares or frowns.

That evening we started playing football on the lawn with extra loud shrieks and laughter with no Shobadi to shut us up. We were in the midst of the boisterous game when we saw Shobadi walking up the drive. We couldn't believe our eyes and stopped dead in our tracks rooted to the ground, mouths open.

Ma and other guests ran to meet her. She looked exhausted, totally distraught, bent with pain. "What happened?" they asked anxiously. "Oh Charudi," she wailed falling into ma's arms. "Our taxi met with an accident." "Thank God, you are safe and sound," said ma happily, hugging her. "The taxi plunged down the hillside, I managed to scramble out in time but all my bottles of *achar* are gone. Charudi, they are gone, broken to bits." she sobbed bitterly, absolutely heartbroken.

Magnolia

Off and on we had tenants staying in our outhouse, Monjula ii. They did not interest me unless they had children of my age group. I found the new lot, that came once, very intriguing They were not the usual locals or people from the plains but *Khampas* from Tibet.

I had heard many tales about the *Khampas*, the warrior race of Tibet. Tall, strong, men fearless and brave always ready to defend their country and people against all odds. They always carried long swords, their only dependable weapon, which they used with great dexterity to lop off heads with a single swift, clean stroke. Men of few words, they put an end to all arguments with their swords. I was a bit nervous and worried to have them living in such close proximity. Silently, they might chop off our heads one day, and nobody would ever know why.

Two strapping young men arrived with a woman and a small child to occupy the house, I was very curious about them but didn't dare to go anywhere near. I would watch them from a safe distance, my bedroom window, which overlooked the outhouse and the garden.

The two hefty men clad in *bokhus*, tramped around in their knee-high Tibetan boots. Their long straight swords in silver sheaths never left their sides. Strong silent men with long sun-burnt handsome faces looked alike. The woman, tall too, by Tibetan standards, was stockily built. She wore her black hair in a long thick plait, which dangled down to her wait or entwined around her head.

They looked different from the Tibetans, I was used to seeing in Kalimpong. The three of them and the child spent the whole day under a small tent pitched on their lawn. At sundown they would go into the house to sleep.

I was very curious about these people and their strange habits. Who were they? Where did they come from? Why were they languishing in Kalimpong? Was a big mystery which couldn't be unraveled because they could only speak their particular dialect and nothing else. Nobody came to visit them and they hardly went out.

Ma tried to befriend them but to no avail. She tried everything possible to get through to them even sign language but all she could get out of them was a shy display of strong white teeth. They were as impervious as the stones in our garden.

They were nature's children. They woke up with the sun and went to sleep at sundown. They enjoyed sitting all day in the open air, light breezes ruffling their hair, swaying branches of trees above, the flowers, the birds, the cicadas all lulled them to a peaceful calmness. Perhaps they hated the restriction of the four walls of a house. They preferred the freedom of wide open spaces. Enjoying nature in all its moods and glory.

These fierce warriors turned out to be the kindest and gentlest of men when they played and gamboled with the little girl or our dog Millie. Once, a nestling fell out of its nest from a tall tree, one of the men picked it up gently from the ground, climbed the tree with great agility in spite of his big cumbersome boots, *bokhu,* dangling long sword and put the little mite back into the nest tenderly. Mission completed, he jumped straight down from his high perch nimbly and landed neatly on the ground.

Inside the rough, tough exterior, lay a childlike simplicity. Simple men untouched by the false characteristics and pretensions of the civilized world.

There was the father, mother and a little girl but it was hard to tell who was the actual father out of the two men. Both men showed equal affection towards the child. Polygamy being the way of life in Tibet, I concluded that the two men were brothers married to one woman.

It was difficult to believe that the child belonged to them at all. She didn't resemble them. The little girl about three, always clad in a *bokhu,* had a long straight nose, a tiny mouth. Her hands and feet were slim and long. A delicate child with the most unusual creamy, flawless skin with the slightest hint of yellow, the colour of a magnolia. She looked refined and dainty unlike her parents or other bouncing Tibetan children who were healthy with rosy cheeks.

My imagination ran wild. May be she was a princess or a daughter of a noble family, entrusted to these loyal *Khampas* to smuggle her out of Tibet because of political trouble there so she should live and bloom into a beautiful Magnolia. I named her Magnolia.

I watched her playing in the garden, a carefree child, running after the techni-coloured butterflies or trying to catch the fluffy balls of chicks, her funny squirming face, as one of her fathers caught a ball of fluff and held it against her cheek.

My fear and apprehension about these people gradually evaporated as I watched them from the safety of my bedroom. I hated small children but this little one drew me like a mesmerized moth to a light. I started going down to the tent for the sheer pleasure of watching this child in action at close quarters. The parents always greeted me with their standard shy smiles.

Magnolia, at first hid behind the broad back of one of her fathers and peeped at me over his shoulder as he sat in the sun. She was not shy or afraid of me but a strange unfamiliar face called for caution. To put her at ease I completely ignored her. My repeated presence broke all her barriers and soon she became my constant companion.

She would wait for me patiently to come back from school on my white horse so that she could take a little ride with me around the compound. In the evenings she would take my hand and walk around. Her bright eyes fixed on my face jabbering nineteen to the dozen. All baby talk, double Dutch to me.

One afternoon she was not waiting for me as usual. There was so sign of the trio either. Alarmed I went into the house. There was no one there but I heard subdued monotone of Tibetan prayers from the bedroom upstairs.

I ran up. There in the master bedroom, on the big bed lay a pale Magnolia, eyes shut hardly breathing. The parents were sitting on the floor while a Tibetan Lama chanted prayers. Incense filled the room and butter lamps burned steadily on the mantle-piece.

I whispered her name hoping desperately she would open her sparkling eyes but her eyelids remained shut, pale and translucent as a wet white rose petal. Her magnolia hue a waxy white.

I was shocked to see her condition. The charming little bundle of energy reduced to an inert heap. "She needs a doctor," I whispered to the grim faced parents. They understood the word doctor, and nodded their heads. I ran to ma and asked her for advice. She told me to call Dr. Boral at once.

The doctor soon arrived. I led him to Magnolia. One look at her and he said gravely, "I don't think she will survive." I didn't believe him, didn't want to believe him. He prescribed some medicines and left. I slept fitfully that night, dreaming of Magnolia walking hand in hand with me, her bright eyes lit up, her expressive face happy. She had a bright aura around her.

Next morning, as soon as I woke up, I ran to the window and drew back the curtains. Tears welled up in my eyes and flowed freely down my cheeks as I looked out and saw Magnolia's forlorn, little empty *Bokhu* drying on the line.

Gallery

Me on my Tattu

Moina and Me

Sunkumari Didi and Me

Phuphu - Centre; Sunkumari - Behind; Mulukchand - Right

MA. Mr. M.C. Pradhan Lady Mountbatten

Burma Raja with his kill

Jamai Babu

Me as a Tramp

Prine Peter

About the Author

Monila De was born in Calcutta and came to live in Kalimpong as a little girl. She has spent most of her life in Kalimpong. The most memorable years of her life, her childhood, she spent in her beloved home Monjula. This house, her paradise, was burnt down during the Gorkhaland agitation which left her heart broken.

In this book she has vividly recorded her child hood experiences right from the British Raj to the late fifties. All these stories have been published in leading news papers and magazines.

She is an avid traveller and has visited almost every country in the world but cannot think of living anywhere else but in her enchanting Kalimpong.